WAR ON THE STEPPES

Three Accounts of the Russians and the Turks

1588 – 1683

Translated by G. F. Nafziger

War on the Steppes: Three Accounts of the War Against the Turks, 1588 - 1683
Translated by George F. Nafziger
Cover design by Vincent Rospond
This edition published in 2019

Winged Hussar Publishing, is an imprint of

Pike and Powder Publishing Group LLC

1525 Hulse Rd, Unit 1   1 Craven Lane, Box 66066
Point Pleasant, NJ 08742   Lawrence, NJ 08648-66066

Copyright © Winged Hussar Publishing, LLC
ISBN 978-1-945430-78-7
LCN 2019931652

Bibliographical References and Index
1. History. 2. Poland. 3. Renassiance

Pike and Powder Publishing Group LLC All rights reserved
For more information on Pike and Powder Publishing Group, LLC,
visit us at www.PikeandPowder.com & www.wingedhussarpublishing.com

twitter: @pike_powder
facebook: @PikeandPowder

Table of Contents

Europe 1560

Zamoyski's Campaign Against the Tartars

FORWARD TO THE 1859 EDITION

The booklet that we are reproducing here was initially published in 1590 in Lyon and them immediately afterwards in Paris. It was unknown to Polish bibliophiles and we have every reason to presume it existed as only the single copy, which good fortune of a public sale has brought into our hands. At the moment when these writings were printed in France, there was the danger of a great imminent war had threatened Poland for a year and the Republic was energetically preparing to face it. The Diet of 1590, held at Warsaw in March, enthusiastically voted for extraordinary subsidies, and, moreover, authorized a loan of 1,500,000 florins, an enormous sum for those days. The great Zamoyski, whose name appears on the title of this pamphlet, deposited the keys of his treasures to the service of the Republic, inviting the senators to follow his example, and placed himself at the head of the nobility, who had courageously earned their illustrious swords in the Muscovite campaigns. It appears, however, that it was thought wise and prudent to awaken the attention of the European States, and particularly that of France, to the danger threatening Christianity. This explains the appearance of this brochure in the two largest cities of France and in the French language. The name of Jan Zamoyski was no stranger in this country. He began his studies in Paris and he was the one who had decided the election of Henry III. He had been distinguished among the Polish ambassadors who had come to seek the chosen king. Distinguishing himself during the wars of Báthory, his name said a great deal and he was put forward as a candidate. France, while saluting the accession of Henry IV, might, notwithstanding its internal troubles, not be deaf to the noise of danger.

Fortunately, everything was confined to the invasion of the Tartars, vigorously repulsed, the details of which this pamphlet relates. The warlike awakening of Poland, the name of Zamoyski, the intervention of the English ambassador at Constantinople and the rich presents distributed among the members of the Divan, brought the sublime Porte back to the politics of peace with Poland, as she should never have given up the reciprocal happiness of the two states. The storm dissipated.

4 War On The Steppes

In the reprint of the old pamphlet, we add a French translation of Jan Zamoyski's speech, at the diet held in 1590, when the danger of the war with Turkey still existed in all its intensity. At that time, while Europe was making rapid material and administrative progress, Poland alone maintained the tradition of free speech and individual citizen action in public affairs. It will therefore be of interest, we believe, to be able to view the Grand Hetman of the Crown at the moment when he exercised his senatorial functions. To allow one to better understand his speech, we will attempt to retrace here, in a few words, the principal points of his noble life, as well as the position of the parties, at the moment when he spoke.

Jan Zamoyski was born in 1543, the same year that Kopernicus died. Thus, on this date, hanging so to speak, the two most magnificent links of the chain of Polish glories. After finishing his studies at Padua, Zamoyski was already a well-known man. He obtained the honor of managing the Youth Rectorate, to which the whole of Europe sent its best to this celebrated academy. Here is one of the indications of its superiority - Fallopio, the famous professor of Padua, had just died and his colleague, Sigonius, was supposed to deliver a eulogy in praise of the deceased when a sudden illness prevented it. It was a 20-year-old Pole who will replace him. Without having time to prepare himself, Zamoyski, gave a discourse, which was admired and printed the next day, in addition to verses in praise of the young orator. Among the merits of Fallopio, Zamoyski did not forget to show his sympathy for the Polish nation:

"Obstat mihi qui dem," he said, *"acerrimus orationis adversarius, dolor; verum committere non possum quin id faciam, quod summum illud in gentem Polonam Gabrielis Fallopii studium amicitiae a me poscrit et flagitat."*[1]

Returning to his country, he was presented to Sigismund Augustus and the young scholar was commissioned by the King to put the archives of the kingdom in order. This hard work gave him a solid knowledge of the affairs of his country and trans-

---

[1] He stands to give it, most energetic speech opponent consumer; it is true, but I cannot commit the will not, as a nation, Poland occurs in the Supreme Good, or the study of friendship from me, poscrit Fallopii of Gabriel, and she asks. "

formed the academician into a man of State. Having lost his father, a senator of the republic, Zamoyski, in announcing this loss to the King, could not restrain his tears, and it was astonishing to see Sigismund-Augustus wiping the eyes of the favorite secretary with his own handkerchief.

After the death of the last of the Jagiellon, Zamoyski, although a simple starosta of Belz, but raised by the vigor of his soul, succeeded in resolving, amidst uncertain opinions, the question of the interregnum. He spoke out in favor of common sense in the election of kings, a form which in the future prepared the fall of the Republic, but then attractive by its simplicity. Proposed in a tumultuous assembly, it was accepted with enthusiasm, and now regarded as the palladium of the liberals of the Republic. From that time Zamoyski enjoyed immense popularity. He carried with him, thanks to the triumph of his proposal, the election of Henry III, and became the soul of the embassy which went to seek him in Paris.

Soon after Stephan Báthory sat on the throne of Poland, he recognized the full value of Zamoyski. He was quickly appointed Grand Chancellor, then Grand Hetman of the Crown[2], and, what was even more important, the intimate friend of the King. In the sanctuary of this noble friendship, cemented by the community of the highest sentiments, there germinated the most glorious future for Poland. In order to prepare and assure it, the two chronic dangers which threatened the security of the country and delayed the progress of its civilization were dried up before their very sources: the incursions of the Muscovites and those of the Tartars on the other. The war against Russia was always very popular in Poland, but the taxes to pay for it were not. But when Zamoyski spoke the purses were loosened. His energy and superior intelligence deployed in the middle of battles and diets produced success every time. The campaigns against Ivan the Terrible succeeded beyond all expectations and manifestly showed the power of Poland. Muscovy lost 200,000 dead and 40,000 prisoners taken to Poland in this war. It was forced to cede to the Republic the rich province of Livonia with its ports on the Baltic. A further coup, and it would have been reduced

[2]Commander of the Crown forces. The Army was made up of Crown forces of the Kingdom of Poland and a separate force of the Ducal forces of Lithuania.

to impotence forever. But on another side, the suppression of the Tartar invasions presented more complicated difficulties. The incursions of these hordes, frequently beaten back with great losses, but never completely suppressed, had tarnished the glory of the Jagiellonian. They retained the most fertile provinces of Poland, Ukraine, and Podolia through force of arms, in the state of uncultivated steppes, and rendered sterile the advantages of the neighboring sea. The continual wars of the nobility in this region as were little more than bloody hunts without resolution. It was well thought that the Cossacks should be allowed to settle and take root in these lands, to have them permanently oppose the Tartars; but this remedy became, afterwards, more fatal than the evil itself.

It is clear that King Báthory and Zamoyski agreed that, in order to permanently protect Poland from Tartar incursions, there was no other way than to invade their den and to incorporate the Crimea into the domain of Republic. It was true, that Poland would have to carry the whole burden of a war with Turkey, which was then seen in Europe, as the most formidable power; so the Jagellonian kings had always retreated from this danger. But Báthory felt strong enough to brave a war with Turkey. The war of Muscovy was but the beginning of the execution of a vast plan. Báthory began negotiations on this grave subject, in Europe and Asia. On two occasions, he sent one of his secretaries, Broniowski[3], into Crimea, to reconnoiter the country and draw up a map. He discussed and arranged all the details of this enterprise with Zamoyski. The Polish army, battle hardened after its war with Muscovy, after having secured the northern frontiers, was to move south and cross the Danube. The sudden death of the King Stefan, however, fatally impaired all that his daring thought had conceived, and which his force could have accomplished. Zamoyski, the sole heir of his projects, saw everything destroyed as if by a bolt of lightning. Other urgent matters, however, drew his attention. In the interregnum, he exercised dictatorial authority. He decided the election in favor of Sigismund III, dispersed the opponents under the walls of Cracow, advanced against Maximilian, the Archduke of Austria before Byczyna, took him prisoner, and placed him in Sigismund's hands, after he had secured

---

[3]Marcin Broniowski (early 16th centuy to 1587)

Sigismund's claim to the throne. Sigismund, a young man of 21 years, without experience, raised by the Jesuits, timid in spirit, but firm in character, taciturn like the prison where he was born, recognized in the depth of his soul Zamoyski's great merits. He took no direct action against him; but he was far from having the useful and voluntary weakness of Louis XIII. He felt the right and the duty to be king according to his own ideas, and in truth he had an excellent foundation. In the course of his reign he went bravely through stormy moments, securing Poland's dominance in the north, living slandered, and dying regretted by the national. From the very beginning of his reign, Sigismund made himself conspicuous by the independent selection of his intimate counselors, and resolutely retreated before the imposition of a pedagogue[4], as was said on the address of Zamoyski:

Rex, e contrario, qui nullius super auctoritatem suam, esse voluit gravem sibi, multaque rerum gestarum fiducià elatum (Zamoisium) imperanti magis quam servienti simile, et veluti additum severum paedagogum, fastidire incipiebat; mox ambienti, et totius pene imperii curam ad se trahere cupienti, aemulos opposuit, invisios eoque graviores." [5]

Among Zamoyski's antagonists, one finds, in the front rank, all the partisans of the House of Hapsburg, who he had, on three consecutive occasions, reduced to silence; afterwards came the Zborowski family, breathing only vengeance, for the death of Samuel, who had killed by the executioner's hand, rightly and legally, with the usual Polish rigor. Finally, conscientious

---

[4]Zamoyski did not hesitate to speak too lightly of the King. At his first interview with him, he was struck with his coldness and his impassivity. "It was well worth it," he whispered to his friends, "that he had gone through the seas to bring this dumb man down." He wrote on March 4, 1588 to Zebyrydowski: "It is said that with me the king is terrified. But, by God is he a king or a kid? This was too strong for Monsigneur de Vislica, who in his youth, being spoiled by his mother, had become accustomed to distribute, among his comrades, all the weapons of the house's arsenal at nightfall, so that they might defend him from the devil, "Such remarks, though repeated in the circle of his friends, pierced without, and did not contribute to push the enraged republicans to the revolt, which soon broke out after the death of Zamoyski, on July 3, 1605.

[5]Kobierzycki, Historia, p. 45., King, on the other hand, who needs the authority to be decided heavy that many exploits the trust wave (Zamoisium) commands rather than serving the same, and the like added to the stern disciplinarian, he began to tire; Soon encompassing nearly the entire government to take care of pull wanted to emulate it poses, hated so much more dangerous. "

citizens, but too anxious for equality, allowed themselves to be carried to a vote of ostracism against that man who had risen so high and made himself feared even by his virtues and his services. The parties were harassing each other and slandering each other reciprocally. It was said against the King, that during the last interview at Revel, with his father Jan, King of Sweden, he secretly negotiated the abandonment of the Polish Throne, in favor of the Archduke of Austria; while, on the other hand, Sigismund repeated dissatisfaction with Zamoyski, plotting to render him useless and put himself in his place. It was under the influence of these feverous dispositions that Zamoïski presented himself before the Diet of 1590. He saw powerful adversaries there who breathed hatred; but, armed with the knowledge of his merits and his love of the homeland, he sensed behind him the support of the nation.

As Grand Chancellor and Grand Hetman of the Crown, he knew how to exercise the two highest positions of the Republic, for the best results using the resources that his political foresight and the splendors of devotion gave him. In the military and civil order, he took away two crowns and justified the legend of his medal: *utraque civis*. The institution of high courts of appeal, hitherto unknown in Poland; foundation of two fortresses, one at Zamosc, the other at Szarygord, in Podolia, on the borders of Turkey; Establishment and staffing of an academy at Zamosc; constant and sympathetic protection given to the letters and to those who devoted themselves to it; colonization of the steppes; encouragement given to industry and commerce; they were truly extraordinary services, apart from his official duties and inspired solely by a love as ardent as his vigilance to the public good. But his virtue par excellence, which crowned all the others, was the high ideal of the homeland, of which he deduced and modeled in himself the sublime type of the citizen, which he showed by his example, absorbing all the aspirations of a Pole. He rejected with pride these bastard titles which foreigners claimed his vanity sought. In the eyes of the great Zamoyski, the title of Polish citizen was worth all, led to everything, and sufficed to the highest ambition, the person is just the result of this. It was from these imperious convictions that the *splendid apeccata* of his life were derived. But also, by this he became the idol of his contemporaries, and remains a great man in history. It is by this that we may regard him as a legislator, *dantem jura*, for the disastrous pocks of the homeland. It is by invoking these noble principles rooted in the Polish hearts after his example that one of the Potockis, in 1794, at the time when all the institutions of the Republic were about to collapse, had it engraved under his portrait: "We shall never cease, being citizens of Poland.

Charles Sienkiewicz

Jan Zamoyski (Anonymous 1604)

NOTES ON THIS 2019 EDITION

The name of the original work was *La deffaicte des Tartares et Turcs*. The particular edition used was published in 1859, and as you can see from the publishers forward was a reprinting of a work originally published in 1590. It appears that the title of that original work was *Vraye Relation de la Route et Deffaicte des Tartares et Turcs par les Polonoais*. [*True Account of the Rout and Defeat of the Tartars and Turks by the Poles*]. This work was presented in its original spelling and grammar.

The forward and speeches at the end of the work presented no issues in translation, but the original work pre-dates the standardization of French, which the *Académie français* began in 1635. As a result, it presented some difficulties. As is common in such works, spellings are what might be called creative, by modern standards. The grammar was inclined towards long, run-on sentences. Because of this, parts of it were rewritten to present a clear representation to the modern reader of what the author intended to say.

The basic work is of particular interest, as it is one of the earliest works published for general consumption by the reading public. In the 16th century, however, only about 2% of the population was literate, so very few copies of this work ever existed. By the time the document used in this translation was printed, apparently only one copy remained. This gives the basic work a unique place in the history of Poland.

In a modern context, Zamoyski is viewed favorably as a counterweight to the dynastic concerns of the Vasa king, who was viewed by some of the nobility, as trying to institute an absolute monarchy in Poland-Lithuania. In fact, the campaign against the Tartars did not go as favorably as this text would indicate, but Zamoyski did go on to carry out successful campaigns against the Swedes, the Hapsburgs and the Ottomans.

TRUE ACCOUNT OF THE ROUT AND DEFEAT OF THE TARTARS AND THE TURKS BY THE POLES

From the crowning of the Serene King of Poland, Sigismund III, done at Krakow, in the month of December 1587, the day of Saint John the Evangelist, in the Church of Saint Stanisław, with great applause, the universal consent of the kingdom and assent of the people, and especially an incredible multitude of the nobility. This included the Cossacks, bellicose and valiant soldiers, a bold and indomitable nation, most of whom are exiled and part for the exercise of the military art, which remain within the confines of Poland, continually damaging the Turks, Tartars, and other people; in this insolence tormenting the circumcised peoples. What has been said since the coronation, that by their proper movement and boldness, raids were made against the Turks and Tartars, and they entered the country of the Turks at the fortress of Oczakow[1], which they dismantled and sacked, and, among other things, they seized 30 pieces of artillery, and set fire to Techinia Castle[2], along with all the country of Moncastro[3], and killed many

---

[1]Ochakiv-Oczakow, a coastal city on the shore of the Black sea, on the territory which had belonged, from 1386, to Poland, and formed part of the vast possessions of the Sieniawski, Jazlowiecki, Buczacki, and other families. A Polish geographer of the 16th century, who visited this port, called it Dassow, the name now taken by the city of Odessa. Poland, then thinly populated, could not colonize these maritime lands. Its kings, to assure the Tartars they would be good neighbors, gave them the right of pasturage on the steppes, which were brought, little-by-little, under the protection of Turkey, in right of possession, which facilitated their predations on Poland.

[2]Techinia-Tiahinia, a military colony, and Krzemenchuk, Upsk, Herbediow-Rog, Missurin, Koczakos, and Barhun were castles raised by the dukes of Lithuania along the Dnieper to hold the Crimean Tartars at bay, which then recognized these dukes as their lords.

[3]Moncastro-Moncastrum. Ackerman, in Turkish, Bialogord or Bilhorod-Dnistrovski in Slavic, a sea port at the mouth of the Diester and on the right bank. It was the principal

people, besides taking many prisoners, and not content with this, they captured ship loaded with merchandise, which came from Constantinople, which they burned after having plundered it, and killed all who were in it.

In July of 1589 the Cossacks continued their enterprises, passing with a large number of men, over a river and into the land of the Tartars, where they arrived in a good land called Coslouu[4], and which they attacked. After they pillaged about 300 shops and amassed a great booty, they killed all that they found and set the city afire.

This greatly irritated the Tartars and in reason they assembled 70,000 horses to gain their vengeance for the injury and damage received from the Cossacks. Incited and pushed by the Turks, the Grand Caro[5], their lord, by the command of whom they crossed the Boristene River, and encamped between Tarnopol, Janopoli, and Zbarazh.

On 18 August, they came out of their camp.

They had divided their army in two parts, moving towards Leopoli (Lwow), the principal city of Rossie (Russia), cruelly damaging and ravaging all the fields and villages, taking prisoner all who fell in their hands, both men and women, great and small, gentlemen or commoners.

The illustrious Lord Jan Zamoyski, Grand Chancellor and Grand Hetman of the Crown of Poland was advised of these raids by the Tartars in Rossie, and the great devastation that they were making in this province. With his accustomed diligence and foresight, after having gathered a large number of men, in the short period allowed to him, he moved, as if flying, to the city of Leopoli, which he had fortified in such a manner as it could defend itself against the Tartars. This done, he passed over the river

port for the transit of Polish wheat. Mahomet II, after the capture of Kaffa, occupied Bialogrod in 1474, and from that time its commerce fall into declined. A caravan route passed from Bailogrod to Oczakow. It was along this route that the Cossacks took their greatest booty. Vis-à-vis Bailogrod, on the left bank of the Dniester, there was a Polish port called Koczubeiow. Długosz reported that in 1415 the Jagellon King, ceded to the requests of the Patriarch and Emperor of Constantinople to load wheat in this port as a gift for the starving city.
[4]Coslou-Koslow-Eupatoria. A name very familiar to the readers of the newspapers during the last war with Russia. It can be found under its Slavic name in the description and on the map of the Crimea made in 1579 by Broniowski.
[5]Caro; the name given by the Slaves to the Tartar Khan.

to prevent the Tartars from further damaging the kingdom and so since His Illustrious Lord still feared that the Turks, though not planning to enter into Poland, then had a large army in Wallachia (as will be discussed later), sent a valiant captain with a good number of men to Camegnezze[6], a city and fortress of great importance on the frontiers, in order that it too might be prepared to defend itself.

While His Illustrious Lordship was seeking to amass men and put in order the greatest army possible, and which this important affair required, the captains and all the nobility of Rossie[7], with a great number of Cossacks of various locations, including those from the near the Fortress of Buscho, Goligir, and Halies[8] skirmished and fought the Tartars (who were divided into several squadrons, returning to the place where they were encamped). They killed many Tartars, and more were killed by the villagers, freeing many slaves from the hands of the Tartars, who began to recognize the value of Polish soldiers and repented entering the Kingdom of Poland.

A squadron of Tartars, which numbered 500 men, retired towards Kuropatnikij, to take it by force, where they found in the fortress many peasants with chariots, who had withdrawn there to save themselves. They fought for more than an hour, killing an Alphezo, with one of the first captains of the Tartars, dressed in yellow satin. His death was the cause of the Tartars withdrawing, but shortly afterwards they attacked with their ordinary fury. And after chasing away the villagers, they moved against the gate, with the firm hope of entering without impediment. However, as the fortress was well furnished with artillery and ammunition, those in it began to salute the Tartars with cannon

[6]This would be Jazlowiecki, Sarosta of Sniatyn, who the great general sent with some cannon, ammunition, and a detachment of infantry to reinforce the means of defense of Kamieniec.
[7]The nobility of Russia. Those who are not versed in the history of northern Europe easily confuse the name of Russia, which was carried in the names of several Polish provinces, with the name of Russia Muscovy. This is a great error. It is as if one confused French Brittany with Great Britain. Such geographical confusion naturally produces erroneous deductions. We are fortunate to learn that a French translation of the excellent work of M. Lelewel, Histoire de Lithuanie et de la Russie, will soon be published. This work clarifies the historical mistake that exists on this matter. Also see the work by M. Duchinski: *Zasady Dzieiow Polski*, 1858.
[8]Buscho, Goligir,and Halics should read Guczacz, Gliniany, and Halicz

and volleys of arquebuses. This killed another of the principal Tartar captains as well as a large number, such that the Tartars broke and fled.

Prince Zbaraski[9] with his men bravely defended himself from a similar squadron of tartars that had arrived before the Zbarash fortress, and the battle lasted some time. Over 1,000 Tartars were killed and the rest retired. Lord Pretics[10] with Lord Palatine of Volhynia, seeing the Tartars were put to rout on all sides, they deliberated returning to camp after taking with them all the prey.

On 22 August the Tartars changed their location and encamped a league near Bauvornouv, a fortress where a woman that they had taken prisoner told them that Madame Włodek[11], sister of the Grand Chancellor, had retired. The Tartars desired to have her in their hands and called on the fortress to surrender her to them. If they did, the Tartars said they would leave without doing any damage to the vicinity. The occupants of the fortress refused to surrender her, saying they would rather suffer death after courageously having fought to defend her. When the Tartars heard this, they began to circulate around the fortress and sought to enter it, but a large number of citizens, armed with farm implements such as axes, pitch forks, and scythes boldly repulsed them. The battle lasted a long time and many inhabitants were killed. Seeing that they could no longer resist the Tartars part of the peasants fled towards the fortress and part towards the lake where several peasants and Tartars drowned. The occupants of the fortress, seeing that part of the Tartars was coming against them, while another part pursued the villagers, they began to fire their artillery and fire their arquebuses against them. This killed more than 2,000 of the Tartars and drove them off.

---

[9]Janus, Prince Zbaraski, Palatin of Braclava, Starosta of Krzemieniec, issue of the great family of the grand dukes of Lithuania. A distinguished man of state and war, he distinguished himself in all the campaigns of his time. King Bathory esteemed him greatly. Bathory having granted peace to Muscovy, named Prince Zbaraski his ambassador to receive the oath of the Grand Duke Ivan..

[10]Jacob Potocki, later Castellan of Kamieniec, and subsequently Palatine of Braclaw, from an illustrious family engaged in the wars with the Tartars. His father, having driven back their invasion of 1541, pursued them as far as the Oczakow entrenchments

[11]Mme. Włodek-Elisabeth Zamoyski, sister of the Grand-Hetman, wife of Włodek, Palatin of Belz. At the moment she was surprised in the Baworow Castle, her spouse was in action with the Tartars at Halicz, where he drove them back.

In this action the Tartars killed a valiant and distinguished Polish captain. The Tartars knew of him and tore him to pieces. They ripped his heart from his body, into which they wished to plunge their scimitars, and the irons of their arrows in his blood, so as to glorify themselves because their scimitars had tasted the blood of such a famous and valorous captain.[12]

Three days alter the Tartars moved on Ozinin[13], four leagues from Wallachia, where the Duke Rosan[14] attacked the Tartars and killed about 1,000 of them.

In the meantime the companies of soldiers of Włodek, Temrux[15], and Potocki, all valiant captains, with which there were some Cossacks, under the command of the Grand Chancellor moved against the Tartars who could not find a crossing of the Tire[16], and thus they marched, encountering at a passage called Caraienmij Brod[17], Zasobinit, some of a great lord, and Janda, son of Machetumel, who were accompanied by 6,000 horse. The Poles, separating their army in two, surrounded them, and put them to the sword, along with the lords, and on this day the Turks freed 2,000 Polish slaves.

News of this reached the ears of the Grand Giray, prince of the Tartars, and enraged, he promptly moved with a large number of his men to relieve them, and when he was close to Kamieniec, to deceive the Poles, so that they could not see all of his army, he left part of his army behind a mountain (a ruse never practiced by the Tartars), and with the other part, with great impetuosity and unpredictability, rode around the Polish army.

---

[12]The Tartars had a great motive in assuaging their hatred. The name of Strus served Tartar women to silence their children. This family was among the most valiant knights, knowing no other trade than war against the infidels. A Polish chronicler mentions 20 members of this family, who, died on the battlefield. They family owned several villages in the Ukraine.

[13]Ozinin, read Orynin, a castle on the Smotrycz, whose garrison had as its instructions to block the movements of the Turks and Tartars.

[14] Jan Romanus Różyński, descendent of Narymund, a Lithuanian prince, and the last of his race. He was a violent man, but unequal in his valor. He later distinguished himself in the wars with Muscovy, following the fortunes of Demetrius, called "The False."

[15]Temrux. Temruk Szymkiewicz. A man of the people and of Tartar origin, versed in oriental languages, he exercised the functions of dragoman of the Republic (translator). He also distinguished himself as a soldier and was called, during the interregnum of 1587 to guard the frontiers along Wallachia. The diet of 1598, to compensate him for his services, gave him a rich domain in Samogitia.

[16]Tire, Tyras; the Dniester.

[17]Caraienniy Brod; read Kamienny-Brod.

The Poles, seeing themselves surrounded by such a large army, discussed what to do in such a disadvantageous situation. It was decided to fight the Muslim dogs, in the name of Jesus. Shaking hands, they promised to fight and to use all industry and military art to break the enemy army, or to die, showing no sign of cowardice or perception of fleeing.

The Grand Zaro advanced his soldiers and the Poles attacked with such great courage. In the first assault, the Grand Zero was mortally wounded by an arquebus shot and died some days later. During the battle the Poles killed the following:

Lord Bathikerey, son of Iaseneiouv, captain of 1,000 horse;
Lord Soltan, Saphigerii of Zaro, with whom a few days later the Cossacks had fought at sea, captain of a large squadron;
Lord Kozia, also a captain;
Lord La Jakssu Vlan, a lord quais-equal with Zaro, with his men;
Lord Aliepluriiouv, cousin of the Grand Zaro, with 2,000 horse;
Lord Karain, captain of the Haaski Tartars;
Lord Chir, an important gentleman and brave soldier, with his men;
Lord Caromazaimssi, Aktaczyin, Maemet, Celiuvei.

The Poles were very proud of this success, where they had not only a hope of defending themselves, but in putting the Tartars to flight, which occurred. They saw the Great Zaro's enterprise fail. The Grand Zaro had hidden his wound because he feared that his soldiers would flee. He ordered his men to retire after suffering the loss of about 4,000 soldiers.

The Tartars then withdrew into a forest not far away. The Polish moved up to sweep them out by assault, but as the Tartars had fortified themselves in the woods, in a battle that lasted three days. Finally, it was god's pleasure that the Polish soldiers were victorious, having fought with such zeal and faith against the Dogs. They attacked and killed all of the raiders in the woods, which numbered about 9,000 Tartars. The Poles then set out in pursuit of the rest of the Tartar Army as far as the Dnieper River, where, to save their lives, the Tartars jumped into the river, many drowned, and the rest, after having crossed, fled to the Turkish camp. At this time 10,000 slaves were freed, among whom were found and a Duke, and the rest of the prey taken in Russie by the Tartars. In this manner the Poles discovered what damage the Tartars had done to their land.

The Cossacks, with the nobility of Russie, which were greatly offended by the Tartars, resolved to enter into the lands of the Tartars and avenge themselves for the injuries they had received. In crossing the Tiras River[18] they encountered a large number of Tartars who wished to stop them, but they were all killed. The Poles them took the road to Caffa, formerly called Theodosia, killing all those who fell into their hands, disregarding sex or age, and they also killed the herds and flocks they encountered.

The Grand Turk seeking to remove the Palatin of Wallachia, had sent Beglerbeg Pasha, with a large army, supported by the Pasha General of Hungary. He had sent him a good number of soldiers, so when the force was united it came to 75,000 men. The Pasha arrived in Wallachia and indicated that he was come to change the Palatinate, but he had actually come to assist and join the Tartars in attacking the Polish and entered Russie to seize the fortress of Kamianets-Podilskyi as vengeance for the injuries and damage done by the Cossacks assisted and favored by the Poles. This was later discovered in a letter sent by the Pasha to the Chancellor, dated 10 September, in which he asked the Chancellor to remedy the insolences of the Cossacks, about whom his lord had received many complaints. It continued that he was ordered not to leave Wallachia until the Cossacks were killed or chased out, but that he wished to continue the peace and friendship with the Polish Crown.

---

[18]Tyras, read Borysthenes. The Dnieper.

The Fortress of Kamieniec-Podolski

The Chancellor was advised that the Pasha had crossed the Danube with a very large army, informed the King, who was then at Vilna, and heading for Livonia to visit the King of Sweden, his father, as well as all the Senate and nobility. He exhorted the nobles to take up arms against the enemies of Christianity, as good children of the Republic, and to gather as large a number of men as possible. They were to be sent to Gluviani, where the army was to be assembled.

The nobility, with an incredible diligence and promptness, prepared and but only for good soldiers who were trained in and accustomed to war, and in a short time assembled 50,000 horse and 15,000 infantry, all chosen and who had otherwise shown their valor in the war against Muscovy, under King Stephen, such that the least of them merited leading an army. When they were all assembled, the Grand Chancellor left Glincini, and moved on Wallachia, where he camped 30 leagues from the Turkish army. Then, desiring to know if the Grand Turk had designs on anything within the Kingdom of Poland, he wrote a letter to the Pasha on this affair. The Pasha responded with an amiable letter, reiterating that he had come only to chastise the Cossacks for the damage they had done to the ships of his lord.

While this occurred, the Grand Chancellor remained encamped with his army, as if he was making war. However, the Polish soldiers wished to attack them and enter Wallachia, and with such ardor that only with great difficulty could the Chancellor hold them in check. He advised His Majesty the King and the Senate of this and awaited a resolution on this affair. Meanwhile his army grew daily with many nobles arriving.

The Pasha, perhaps hearing of this, not daring to push into Poland had retired on the Danube, having undertaken nothing in Wallachia. He abandoned his army and topped in Silistra, with only 4,000 men.

Copy of a Letter From Beylerbey Heder Pasha
To the Grand Chancellor
Initially Translated from Turkish into Italian
And from Italian into French (and then English)

Among those who follow Jesus and who love the Christian Faith, the Lord Jan Zamoyski, Chancellor and Grand Hetman of the Crown of Poland, at present in place of the King, Defender of the Poor, Our Great Friend, we wish you good health and prosperity, and offer our good wishes.

First of all, we thank you for your goodwill, which your lordship offers us, and yet we thank you for the good treatment that your lordship has done to Ciaus sent by us, in truth we are not the cause of what followed. The Cossacks, who have done us great evil. If, you had restrained the Cossacks, the Tartars would never have entered your country, and so it would be well for you to send ambassadors to the Emperor, my lord.

I come here not to make war against you or your country, but to see and understand from where these Cossacks come and as you may see that I have not come with artillery, nor with any other war apparatus, having the command of the Emperor, my Lord, that if you wish to send your ambassador before winter, for the confirmation of the peace, that I may guard against all kinds of war, and that the law and your faith forbid us to raise our scimitar against those who have made peace with us, and thus when he shall summon the ambassador to the Emperor, My lord, I take it upon my head that you will obtain everything according to your will.

As an explanation for the first letter from your lordship, I could only with difficulty after four days find an interpreter so now I beg your majesty to write me, that my secretary Mustafa will copy it and your lordship shall sign it, in order that we can read in our language what you have written us with our own eyes. I ask this of your lordship, as my great friend. On this, with my servant friends near you, I recommend myself to the good graces of your lordship, from Heavy to earth. From Baba, 27 October, the year of our great Prophet Mohammed, 900.

In the place of the Emperor, my lord, in all of Rumalia, or true Europe.

Beylerbey Heder Pasha

Speech of Jan Zamoyski

I lack, to the best of my abilities, many of the qualities indispensable to the one who is called to express his opinion on the affairs of the Republic; for he must have a free spirit, a rested heart, and all its faculties available, while in the actual state where by with the permission of God we find ourselves, I am far from being able to enjoy all this. I am far from concerned with the effects of eloquence, in order to excite the directing of passions. There is no need of it in this assembly, where the voice of a senator should not be directed at ornaments, but at the simplicity and usefulness to the council. Now, what makes it difficult for me at the moment is being able to speak without emotion. My heart is not a rock. It is that of a man, tender and sensitive, touched by the adventure in which we find ourselves. Nevertheless, I will do my utmost to present the means of securing both the defense of the Republic against its external enemies, and its internal pacification.

I am struck first, to hear here about the shortage of Your Majesty's treasury; a bad thing in itself, and harmful to the Republic. I remember having insisted on the necessity of retaining in full the revenues of the late King Stephen, of glorious memory. Your Majesty should have summoned the Grand Treasurer, as well as His Magnificent Lordship. the Archbishop, then other senators and a few nuncios, to settle the accounts, to combine Your Majesty's needs for his table, for his stable, and for his household; and after having provided resources to meet his needs, use for his largesse only the excess of revenue over expenditure. Scarcely had I left Cracow, when I went to the threshold of the royal castle, which I heard immediately around me, that the women of the market, manufacturers, and brewers, were shouting after Your Majesty. I am aware that Your Majesty is not the cause of this serious deficit; Your Majesty is too recently come to Poland to be aware of these affairs. But it is the fault of those who are called to it by their offices. They must explain this to us.

As to the question of Muscovy, I am of the opinion to write the grand duke and ask him why he dares to besiege the castles, which, according to the last treaty, belong to the Republic; and after he has answered, we shall see what is to be done.

The origin of the danger that threatens us on the part of Turkey comes first of all from the delay of the expedition of our ambassador, and consequently from the ineffectiveness of the commission, which I undoubtedly had a part; because I am always ready for any service that my party requires. One must also add the absence of Your Majesty, and consequently the wrong done to the consideration of the Republic and the hostility of the enemy. In the meantime, all the Christian monarchs soliciting an accommodation with the great Turk, no matter what conditions, which we will not do. The King of Spain keeps his ambassador at home. The [Holy Roman] Emperor pays him a tribute, which lately has not been paid in January, as Turkey requires, but in March, so it was necessary to add to the total sum the amount of one month. The Emperor Ferdinand was a powerful monarch and possessed only the states which the House of Austria had just divided, and yet it was only by means of a tribute that he has maintained peace with Turkey.

We are the only ones who maintain peace with Turkey without paying tribute, and we have had to make war three times with Turkey. In Hungary first; then with King Ladislas; thirdly in Wallachia, where King Albert entered and saw his army perish. It is almost impossible for the moment to wait for an accommodation or peace with this enemy. For the demand of a tribute, and other circumstances of which I have spoken before, particularly the demand that was made to our ambassador, to immediately pay 100,000 florins; The advice given him of selling his sable martens to make this sum; the embarrassing surveillance of which he is the object; the refusal of a delay because he was ill for the accomplishment of his mission; all these are not precursors of peace.

Do not bribe us in vain for the hope of foreign aid. All I know of it is that the Pope, full of his paternal benevolence for us, would be glad to help us in this instance. The Abbot Reszka, Your Majesty's envoy, has informed me by his letter, that the Holy Father, preoccupied with the disturbances and upheavals of the Christian kingdoms and states, would be more inclined to maintain peace with Turkey; But if it could not be otherwise, he is quite disposed to assist us, and he has even admitted that it is his duty, when it is a question of a war against the infidels. Abbot Reszka was also administered to the Venetians at the hearing, in which he expressed the danger which threatened us, adding that Venice being a free republic, it must give a special favor to us, [as we are] also free. They replied that they have a great deal to do at home, that they are also threatened on all sides, that they are thus placed between the anvil and the hammer, and are, therefore, unable to assist us. From Austria we have nothing to expect as it is for itself. The King of Spain is quite abrupt by his war with France and England. Some hope might be founded among the Germanic electors; but as they fear that the King of Spain will invade France and become a threat to them, they seek with all their efforts to strengthen the King of Navarre (Henry IV) as much as they can. However, we are linked by ancient treaties with the Elector of Brandenburg, and that of Bavaria, a well as with the Princes of Brunswick and Pomerania. Nothing prevents us from seeking to claim their aid.

But no matter how great the assistance that we might be sure from outside, if discord reigns within us, we cannot be sure of anything, for discord dissolves the strongest armies and brings about the fall of the states. If, to the contrary, we are united within, we may hope that with God's help, the enemy, however powerful it may be, will not overwhelm us. Hannibal had already caused the Romans to suffer three terrible defeats; all bowed their heads before him; only one city, reduced to its walls, resisted him. Meanwhile the Romans, unanimous and devoted, at length saved the city, reconquered what they had lost, and put the enemy to complete rout. It is the discord and the sedition that has delivered Wallachia into the hands of the infidels; it was by this that the Hungarians lost their independence. Discord has always led to the ruin of states.

As to means of defense, I have proposed several of them: ordinary taxes, capitation, the ban, the arrière-ban, and the property tax. Maybe I'll take you far, but it will only bring you back directly to our subject. Our present strength is not great; but those of Alexander the Great, were not superior to ours. His enemy, whom he overcame, was about equal in power to Turkey. At the beginning of the war, he had only 30,000 combatants, and in his war chest, a sum sufficient for half a year. The haughty Persian despised him so much, that he wrote to one of his satraps to seize Alexander, to flog him, and to send him before him. If I speak of it at this moment, it is to remind us that a good organization and a vigorous government lend to a small number of troops sufficient strength to fight against an immense army. This happens most often when the enemy disregards his opponent; which is exactly what happened with Darius concerning Alexander. He succeeded not only in securing Macedonia, but in invading the enemy's dominions, in pushing his conquests there, and in augmenting his troops and war resources as he advanced.

I were to do so, I should be of opinion, not only to go to meet the enemy, but to risk everything, to cross the Danube, and to resolutely tempt fortune. The first happy encounter opens the path to later successes. In the meantime, we must employ all our efforts to increase as much as possible the treasury. When the chest is very full, we shall not lack fighters, and I will answer for it.

The plan of King Stefan[1] was admirable. When he began his expeditions in the Muscovite War, it was to fall upon Turkey with more compact forces, to call for cooperation the enemy of the Sultan, the Persian, and attack the Porte by land and sea. No one suspected such an enterprise. These things were to be kept secret. The Pope, Gregory XIII, having learned that King Stefan was about to begin the war, and a war which might endanger him, inquired solicitously upon which the hope of success might be founded. "Remain calm," replied the King, "I am certain of my facts; I have my reasons and my roads are great and safe; I build on a solid foundation. I have drawn upon the whole plan of the late king. I remember putting it in front of Your Majesty. However, we must not disclose these things, and put it on our path.

What we have to worry about is raising money. Let each of us give what he has, and as much as possible; it is only a question

[1]King Stefan Bathory

of finding the means of assuring to each his share after the peace.
In the extreme case where we are, it is unworthy to think of his
individual affairs. Among the Romans, when they were already
oppressed by the enemy, gold and precious stones were brought
for the defense of the Republic; the women were throwing their
robes and their ornaments at the feet of the generals. Worthy ex-
changes in truth, against an immortal glory. It is quite clear that,
in the midst of public danger, the affairs of private individuals
also fail. The regrets in this case would be moved. I am already
impoverished in the midst of the difficulties which surround us.
I've incurred many expenses. Well, all that remains to me, I give
it and offer it to the Republic, only reserving a part for my main-
tenance. I offer it to the urgency of its needs. I will not hide a
single denier; I will deposit the keys of my modest purse. Nor do
I think of any of Their Lordships will fail to provide for the needs
of the Republic. We must not forget our cities of Prussia, which
have collected immense wealth, both by internal trade and by
that which they do with the Low Countries; it is only necessary to
stimulate them a little, and to assure their advances. As for fire-
arms, gunpowder, and other munitions of war, we shall also be
able to draw them from our cities, as well as those of Germany.

To close this deliberation, I propose to appoint a commit-
tee, composed of members of both houses, to discuss and, after
careful reflection, fix our means of defense, scrupulously keep-
ing it secret. It would be dangerous to give a ruling on this, in
a tumult, and by public discussion, to instruct the enemy to our
detriment. The Archduke Maximilian, an adversary as he is, is
not very dangerous to us. There is something worse, of which we
must be on guard. I implore Your Majesty and Their Lordships,
the senators and other gentlemen, who, in this last shipwreck,
have set themselves against us, not to take too much to heart
what will be said for the common instruction and warning and if
one repeats in a loud voice what is whispered secretly.

There is nothing more pernicious to the Republic than bad
will, suspicion, dissent, and divergence of mind *inter cives reg-
ni*.[2] It is thus that states and governments have perished. We
can fight against arms, and defend ourselves; against venom and
poison, we cannot. It is venom and poison, administered by a

---

[2]"Citizens of the kingdom"

criminal hand; it is precisely what, in a Republic, is discord and dissent, more dangerous than the most formidable enemy. I will therefore say, for Your Majesty's warning, while protesting that I am far from believing these suspicions and insinuations, I will say what strikes my ears. I will say it frankly and freely.

A great defiance, Sire, manifests itself among our citizens. Not only between the citizens individually, but between the state and the state, between power and power, and what is even worse, between servant and master, between the subject and Your Majesty. The other party, and Maximilian himself, speaks loudly, that all that he meditates and does in contravention of our transactions with the House of Austria, he does it *sciente et suffragante Sueco*.[3] These are his own words, his *formalia verba*, it is thus that he addresses Your Majesty.

I continue: The envoy Mustapha on his way back to Your Majesty came to my house. I received him honestly in my house, by giving him hospitality, as is proper for a gentleman. When the conversation began, he congratulated me first, I do not know what, and then he communicated two things to me. The first was that the Emperor his master had announced to King Stephen by the last envoy that at the least hostile movement by the Cossacks, at the first manifestation of any other cause, he would immediately go to war with us; that he was prepared for it and was only waiting for an aggression on our part. As for the second point, he said to me: "Your King is now on a journey to visit his sister, and to give her in marriage to Maximilian, to whom he must also hand over the Crown of Poland."

At these words, I was amazed at hearing such news from the mouth of an infidel. I, a senator, could not believe it. However, I said to myself, the Hungarian, an intelligent man, and well versed the affairs, would not dare to invent such a story. No matter, I took it for a silliness, and I began to laugh, asking him only where he could dig up this story. He replied that it was indeed a reality; that he had it from a person of no small importance, the ambassador of the Emperor Christian himself, who received this news as sure and certain. I did my utmost to deprive him of this vision, telling him that I was quite astonished that he, a serious man, would add faith to lies." Besides," I replied, "you have been

---

[3] "...with the knowledge and support of Sweden"

Christian, you must know the manner in which Christians act. Is it believable that my master, who God, through so many difficulties and dangers, has placed on the throne, would place it at the same time in the hands of his enemy, how is it believable that he would abandon his crown and flee far from us?" t is thus that I have tried to deprive him of all confidence in this fable.

But I will add something more. The Archduke himself immediately after the transaction which he stipulated with us, and after his interview with Your Majesty dared to make the following proposition: "Please," he said, "grant me one thing." "I am," I replied, "at Your Highness's orders, provided that it is fair, and is not prejudicial to our liberties or to Republic, for in that case I am a slave to my faith and duty." "That is not the case," he continued, "only I beg you to help me in a case. I know your fidelity. But what if your master induced you to make me sit down on the throne?" I was exceedingly astonished to see that, being still captive, he could form such projects and still compromise the name of Your Majesty. On this I told him that neither I nor His Majesty, who doubtless thinks of it, cannot commit such an attack in a free Republic. "But," he continued, "you are a Grand Hetman." "Yes," I said, "but the Grand Hetman is bound by his duty and his virtue." In summary, only he had not abandoned his pretensions, but that he trades seriously to make them succeed. He was written demanding the execution of the treaty. He seems to have replied, and his reply must be in the Chancellery of His Majesty; He says that having made an accommodation with His Majesty, one no longer wants to worry about it. *Encore un mot.* At Innsbrück, where there was a conference with some Austrians, the Archduke Maximilian He confessed before the ambassador of one of the princes of the Germanic Corps, that all that he had done against the commission and against the transaction had been in and with the connivance of the Swedish, *sciente et suffragante Sueco*. I know that it is a mere slander that he throws at Your Majesty in order to produce a split between us and Your Majesty. However, this trip of Your Majesty to Revel, as well as the surety given Their Lordships, the senators, who were in the assistance of Your Majesty inspires fears, and an open field to suspicions.

Besides, certain letters from the Muscovite, addressed to Your Majesty's father, affirm that the lords of Lithuania are ready to be accommodated with him, and to remain, as he claims, under his power. The Muscovite, a prompt and fraudulent enemy, has imagined this to cast vexation between us and our brothers in Lithuania, and to quarrel with them. He sees that our strength is in our unity, and especially in our completed pacification (after the troubles of the last interregnum). Let us admit that we have not been sufficiently circumspect on this occasion. I also accept that I had a part in this. I imagined I could overcome the opposing party by clemency and benevolence. It seems that our aim is not attained for turbulent spirits are still rumbling there. It is our fault, it is the consequence of inequality. The whole world knows how this affair has ended, our adversaries, the Pope, the Emperor, and the King of Spain, also know it.

Your Majesty has sent letters of admonition to those who still had to take the oath, to satisfy the conditions of peace and the Emperor's obligations. These letters, to this day, have remained unanswered, non caret suspicione.[4] Fredro brought use the news that the Emperor of Turkey regards with distrust at the treaty that we have concluded with the House of Austria. If this treaty should remain doubtful, by the non-fulfillment of the conditions of the commission, this matter must be taken without delay into a serious consideration. I do not suppose that any one of us here dares to be influenced by the dignity of the Imperial House, when it acts *foedera* which must remain *sacrosancta*. It would be absurd to care for the susceptibility of others, *dignitatem ipsorum induere nostra indignitate*, to cover the honor of someone else with our dishonor.

It is here that it is indispensable to take care of it, and among all other affairs, this is not the least important. In the course of two years, it is was barely six weeks that we happen to be assembled. In the meantime, the weather and the intrigues multiply. We are well aware of the mistakes of this family. There are in Breslau records on which is inscribed the cost Polish experiences. To dismiss this matter, to pass it under the authority of the law, to consider that it would be dangerous to take care of it, no one could possibly be of this opinion except the troublemak-

---

[4]It does not lack of suspicion

ers.

The Germans have a golden bull, which was granted to them by one of their emperors, and it is held that it is only a German who may be elected emperor. On the other hand, another emperor claimed to persuade the Poles that it was only in the West that they should seek their king. Let no one be mistaken on my account and insinuate that the Chancellor is going to give way to ambition. I am not so foolish that I can admit these ideas and amuse myself with these things. I am content with what God has given me. I thank Him that by my honest conduct, being a gentleman, I have not defiled either myself or my house. I am satisfied with that. I am ready to give every necessary guarantee that my ambition does not go beyond. Besides, I am a king. Let me propose such a condition as to be most suitable; I will subscribe. I am a king when I act honestly. *Rex sum, cu recte facio.*[5] For the rest I do not care.

---

[5] I am King, with a straight face

Speech of Sigismund III
(In Response to Jan Zamoyski)

In fulfilling the mission which God has pleased us to entrust to us, it is very important for us to preserve the love and confidence of Your Lordships, which our neighbors are working to destroy. We feel the necessity of making this subject a public declaration, of which we have been absent to this day, in order to be able to produce it in the full Senate. So, we assure Your Lordships that neither we, nor His Majesty our father, have never thought of causing dissension, or doing any practice, with these good neighbors. For in this case we would have shown contempt for the benefits of God, who has placed us on the throne of our ancestors; We would have paid for the attachment of Your Lordships as well as so many exploits and so much spending. God keeps us that this freedom, which Your Lordships hold of our ancestors, be it, by our cause, in what is damaged. It is true that one took steps to obtain the hand of our sister, both with His Majesty our father, in whose power it is, that with us and Her Majesty our aunt, and this through our servants and our senators; But His Majesty our father was no more favorable to this proposal than we ourselves who rejected it. As to what is said, that the Archduke Maximilian affirms that these steps were made with our knowledge and with our connivance, *sciente et suffragante Sueco*, none of the Austrians are in a position to do so. Our trip out of the kingdom was undertaken with the knowledge of all the *Éstates*. If there had been any serious affair, we are certain that Your Lordships would not have suffered the loss of our hereditary kingdom, but quite the contrary, that after having guaranteed the security of the Republic, you would have lent us your assistance. We therefore request Your Lordships not to believe the rumors that have been spread; But rather to believe in love, which we always preserve intact.

King Sigismund III of Sweden Poland-Lithuania, 1556-1633
(Marcello Bacciarelli, circa 1769)

Notes on Polish Russia and Muscovite Russia

The Slavs, who originally inhabited the vast eastern con-
tinent of Europe, constituted several communities, without any
political link between them, and their primitive names were
derived either from their principal towns, from their rivers, or
from nature of their localities. It was only the incursion of the Va-
rangians, a Nordic race, in 860 AD, which imposed on most Slav
countries the common name of Russia, a name which for the most
part was not even known to those who bore it. Their populations,
hitherto occupied only by pacific agricultural labors, were unworthy of war, without any means of resistance, and humbly arranged themselves under the banner of a foreign monarchy, military and conquering. This monarchy, after a glorious existence of
200 years, was dissolved in 1054 AD, at the death of Yaroslav the
Great. For this part of Slavia there remained only the fortuitous
name of Russia, and numerous offspring of the princely family,
who, stimulated by dynastic claims, succeeded only in fighting
without success and without result.

Slavia bearing the name of Russia, having thus resumed
almost the same form of separate communities, that extends
along the western shores of the Dvina and the Dnieper, yielding
either to the pressure of its geographical position, or to the necessity of a protectorate against the Tartars, or to the influence of
a more advanced civilization, of a gentle government, or to the
tradition of the ancient conquests, was gradually incorporated,
now into Poland, After the union of these two nations, it formed
an integral part of the crown of Poland.

A hundred years after the fall of the Emperor of the Va-
rangians, George Dolgoruky, a descendant of this family, inherit-

ed a wild country which did not count as a Russian country, and which was consequently called the land of Suzdal. George, who had been ill-treated by his relatives, constantly repeated that the Russian soil did not bring him happiness, reigned in his domains with an idea of vengeance, the first symptom of which was the foundation of Moscow in 1447 AD.

The learned professor, Mr. Pogodin, offered to the Grand Duke Alexander, the son and presumptive successor of the Emperor Nicholas, when he first entered Moscow, "this little drop became ocean" is the only real nucleus of the Russian Empire. He frankly rejects all other historical deductions and sees everything based on the conquests of Muscovy. His conquests soon spread, and soon the grand dukes of Muscovy pushed the frontiers of their possessions to the banks of the Dvina and the Dnieper. When they came to these rivers, they saw on their opposite banks the same race, but one other nation; the same language, but other ideas; the same religion, but another belief. There they saw princes from the blood of Rurik, but who loved to seek and find glory under the white eagle of Poland. They saw in it the world of aristocracy, which made a parade of incomprehensible enigmas, although in the Russian language: *Dzesti mojei niedam mikomu*: My honor is mine, I yield it to no one.

In vain Muscovy tried to cross these rivers by vigorous efforts. Its ambition found a long halt there, which lasted 400 years. The infamous policy which gave it the passage, soon after opened to it those of the Danube and the Rhine, Peter I, not having in his will restricted, as had Octavius, his empire to these rivers.

There are therefore two Russia's: Muscovite Russia, amalgamated during the centuries with Muscovy, and the Polish Russia, an integral part of Poland; differing from each other by morals, dialect, industry, the customs of their inhabitants, and the very time of their independent existence, touching themselves only with a traditional hatred. Today the Polish peasants hate the Muscovites and call them no other than their real name: "Moskali." They know that the *podouchué* taxes on souls — the *rekroute*, the burial of a living man — the *Knoute*[6], government without mercy — were not known in the time of Poland.

---

[6]The "knout" is a whip used for punishment that frequently caused death.

Many people will be surprised to learn that the names of Cheopicki, Kniazilwicz, grave on the great Arch de Triomphe in Paris, similarly those of celebrated writers Orzechowski, Czartor-ki, Niemecewicz, Miekiewicz, and so many other illustrious Poles are Russian-Polish names

If other proofs of this difference of the two Russias were to be made, which are notorious in the country, it would only be necessary to consult the modern travelers who have wished to pay their attention to them. Besides, we have in our archives a report of Senator Derjavin presented to the Emperor Alexander, where this difference is noted in precise terms.

Poland was necessarily the last among the European states to recognize the sovereigns of Muscovy with their imperial title of "all the Russias," but in order that this title, evidently false and misleading, should constitute for Russia no right in regard to Polish possessions, the Republic demanded, and Catherine II, by the declaration which follows, finds all that can be articulated in the clearest and cleanest way to specify a fact and establish a right.

Recognition of the Title of Empress of All the Russias
By the Polish Republic
On 5 September 1764.

"Whereas the ratification of the declaration presented by the ministers of the Court of Russia, and inserted in the constitutions of the last Warsaw Diet, concerning the title recognized by the Republic of 'the Empress of All the Russias,' confirmed by the seal and by the signature of Her Most Serene Imperial Majesty, was not delivered to us until after the closing of the convocation diet, we have ordered that this same ratification, transcribed according to the original, should be placed among the Constitutions of this election diet. Here is word for word its content:

"*We, Catherine II, by the grace of God, Empress and autocrat of all the Russias, Muscovy, Kiev, Vladimir, Novgorod, etc., let us make everybody in particular and especially to the interested parties, that:*
"*We have sent to the Serene Polish Republic and to the Grand Duchy of Lithuania ministers with our orders and assent, to ex-*

pose and explain our true and sincere thoughts concerning the use we should make of the title of "Empress of all Russias," to which our ministers are satisfied by the following declaration:

"We Hermann Charles Keyserling, Count of the Holy Roman Empire, intimate and actual Councilor of Her Majesty, the Empress of All the Russias, etc., and Minister Plenipotentiary to the Serene Republic, declare by the presents:

"It is well known that the treaty of peace concluded in 1686 between Russia and the Serene Republic of Poland contains an exact enumeration of the countries, provinces, and countries that are and will be in the possession of the two contracting parties, There can be no doubt or dispute on this subject.

"But we often fear what is not to be feared, and this is how we thought we saw a danger in this title: "Empress of All the Russias." In order that all may know and see the spirit of fairness and benevolent disposition of the Empress of All the Russias towards the Serene Republic of Poland and the Grand Duchy of Lithuania, we declare, in reply to the claim addressed to us, That Her Imperial Majesty, our august sovereign, by enacting the title of "Empress of All the Russias," does not intend to assume any right, either for herself, for her successors, or for her empire, over the countries and lands which, under the name of Russia, belonged to Poland and the Grand Duchy of Lithuania; and acknowledging their domination, it offers instead to the Serene Republic of Poland a guarantee or retention of its rights, its privileges as well as the countries and lands that it rightfully or presently possesses, and it promises support and protect it always against anyone who attempts to disturb them.

"We further promise to take care that Her Imperial Majesty, our august sovereign, shall ratify and confirm this declaration in a space of seven weeks and with her own hand. In faith whereof we have signed this deed, and have affixed thereto the seals of our arms.

"Done at Warsaw, 23 May 1764.
"Hermann Charles Keyserling,
"Count of the Holy Roman Empire

"Nicholas, Prince Repnin."

"This declaration being entirely in conformity with our will and our orders, we approve its text in the most solemn manner, ratifying it and signing it with our own hand and having affixed the imperial seal to it. Given in our imperial palace, St. Petersburg, le 9th day of June 1764, the 2nd year of our reign.

"By order of Her Majesty, our certifications as an exact copy.

"N. Panin.
"Prince Alexander Galitzin,
"Vice-Chancellor of the Empire."

"As already in the convocation diet, we have, as the other courts have, but under the reservation of this ratification, acknowledged to the Serene Empress of Russia, the title of "Empress of All the Russias." We recognize the title in question under the reservations expressed therein.

(Collection of documents relative to Russia,Paris, 1854, ini-8, p. 318.)

TWO VIEWS OF THE SIEGE OF VIENNA 1683

Translated by G.F.Nafziger

THE SIEGE OF VIENNA 1683

Translated by G.F.Nafziger

Originally Published:
Toulouse Cologne
Jean Boudet   Jacques le Jeune
1683   1683

Opposite page: Polish winged hussar.

NOTES ON THIS 2019 EDITION

This is a translation of two contemporary accounts of the siege of Vienna. The first presents more of an overview that begins with the issues between the Holy Roman Empire and France, which weakened the Empire, and the ongoing difficulties between the Porte and the Empire.

The second work is an account of a Frenchman who spent the siege inside the walls of Vienna and relates what he saw and heard.

The first work is *Relation de tout ce qui s'est passé en Allemagne depuis la descent des Turcs en Hongrie jusques à la siege de Vienne* [A Description of Everything That Happened in Germany From the Invasion of the Turks into Hungary to the Siege of Vienna] (Cologne: Jacques le Jeun, Marchand Librairie, 1683). It is anonymous. The second work contained herein was François, *Relation du Siege de Vienne Mis par les Turcs le quinsieme Juillet* [Account of the Siege of Vienna Undertaken by the Turks on 15 July]. (Toulouse, Jean Boudet, 1683).

The first work, *Relation de tout ce qui s'est passé en Allemagne*, was written in an older style of French, a form that predates that established by the *Academie française*, so the translation was not a simple process. Aside from spelling issues, at times the meanings of the words used by the author are slightly different from those of modern French. This author's use of accents was amusingly confused and inconsistent.

The second work, *Relation du Siege de Vienne*, had the same linguistic and grammatical issues of the first, but more so. In addition, the quality of the print was not very good, the ink had seeped through the pages so one page could be seen in shadow on the backside of that page, and there were blotches which occasionally obliterated words.

In translating *Relation de Siege* I found the author's style very difficult to translate literally, as his style was awkward and would not have been comprehensible had I done so. As a result, I was frequently obliged to make sense of his sentences and completely rewrite them.

This work is particularly interesting in that it is written by an individual who was in Vienna during the siege and he describes what life was like in the city during the siege. To say that it is a primary source document would be an understatement. - GN

Jan Sobieski, King of Poland-Lithuania – 1629 – 1696. (Jan Tricius, 1680)

Account of What Has Happened in Germany
From the Descent of the Turks into Hungary
To the Raising of the Siege of Vienna.

The Emperor had hoped that in signing the Peace of Nijmegen[1] that France would content itself with the advantages it had gained in the war. But France's continued successes had only inflated its courage; scarcely had it signed the treaty, then it thought of breaking it. The Emperor was greatly distressed by this conduct, since, on the other hand, he was threatened by the Turk, and was not sufficiently confident of his strength, to believe that he could resist these two powers at the same time. He dispatched Count Albert de Capara to the Porte with attractive proposals in the hopes of continuing the truce that existed between the two empires, and which was soon to expire. Meanwhile the partisans of France took it upon themselves to attack his conduct, publishing that he was more careful to accommodate himself with the infidels than with the King of France, from whom, nevertheless, he could hope for great assistance. But they did not say that at the same time, France did not want an accommodation of him except on conditions which dishonored not only the Empire, but that would produce the ruin of the Emperor. The King of France wanted all his violations of the Peace of Nijmegen to be approved by a single treaty, which he justified by certain claims that I should call ridiculous, which I will not, however, as one must have respect for everything that comes from the crowned heads.

Be this as it may, the Emperor was anxiously awaiting news from Capara, where his ambassador, deceived by the tricks of the Grand Vizier, who was happy to keep him occupied with hopes of peace, while he thought of nothing but war, told him that he thought he was coming to the end of the negotiations. This filled the Emperor and his whole court with joy.

---

[1] A series of treaties signed between August 1678 – December 1679 that ended various wars between France, the Dutch Republic, Spain, Brandenburg, Sweden, Denmark, the Prince-Bishopric of Münster, and the Holy Roman Empire.

In fact, though the Emperor might have wanted to take up arms against this common enemy of Christianity, he still knew the plans of France, which conspired for some time against the Empire, the concerns of his house was to regard France as a much more dangerous enemy than the Turk, who demanded only a fortress or two, whereas the other wanted to swallow everything up.

A rumor spread in the month of January that the King of France had encamped 50,000 men along the Saône and almost to the Saar. This obliged the Emperor to protect the Rhine which meant that there was nothing more than patrols on the border with Turkey, because he preferred to strip Hungary of men than to expose his lands to an invasion by the French. Count von Mansfeld, who was his representative to the King of France, had orders, to observe everything that occurred in the French Court, whereas they took pleasure in giving him new fears every day. Because of this he could only report what was said, knowing that the King said he would invade Germany the next spring if the Emperor did not grant him everything he demanded.

Besides, whatever I have just said here, which is far removed from my subject, relating to the success of this war, which the Turks had just launched against the Empire. However, it is necessary to examine this and show what the Emperor had reason to fear from the French, so that he should not be blamed if he did not employ all his strength to repel the Turks from the start. It is not inappropriate to say, setting the issue of religion aside, that the Emperor had more interest in opposing France than the Turks. This is because the House of France was actively seeking the ruin of the House of Austria. Be that as it may, the Emperor, seeing that the fact was far removed from the hope he had conceived from Capara's promises, he raised new levies of troops in all the Hereditary Provinces and solicited the Christian princes to join him against this common enemy of Christianity. The King of Poland formed an offensive and defensive league with him. Many other princes promised him assistance, some of men, others of money, and then they prepared for war, seeing that it was impossible to avoid it. However, as Rome knew what was happening in France, the Pope sent a letter to the King of France, where, after having given him all the qualities that are due to a great prince, as he really is, exhorted him to want to assist the Emperor, or at least not to prevent others from assisting him.

The Emperor worked to fortify Vaag and Raab, and gave the Hungarians the responsibility of protecting them, hoping that as they acted to defend not only their goods, but their women and children, that they would rather kill one after the other, than to flee before the enemy.

They also fortified Raab and Commore, which were like the boulevards of Christianity. Because one thought that the Turks would never leave two fortresses of such importance behind them to move to besiege Vienna, less attention was paid to the fortifications of Vienna, such that when the Turks arrived, there was still some rubbish in the city's moats and some ruins in a bastion. Nonetheless, they attempted to repair all this under the cover of their cannon and musketry, which prevented the Turks from coming to harass the workers, as they would have wished. But what facilitated its execution was the fact that the Turks could not bring their cannon by the Danube, because of Raab and Commore, which were still held by the Emperor, and it took them a long time to bring them to Vienna overland, the roads being broken up in many places, which prevented them from being able to arrive quickly.

But to speak of things in chronological order, I shall say that the Emperor seeing that the Turks had raised the horse tail[2], which was for them the signal for war, and that otherwise the number of hostile acts on the frontier had risen, he held a council of war and resolved to anticipate their plans. It was resolved in the council that they would bring out the troops from their garrisons and give them a rendezvous a league from Pressburg, to march from there on Neuhausel (Nové Zámky), which they hoped to besiege in the hopes that it would be taken before the Turks could secure it.

Command of the army was given to the Duke of Lorraine, because, of the confidence which the Emperor had in him. Using him eliminated the jealousy of many other commanders who had not been content had they been obliged to obey someone other than the brother-in-law of the Emperor. Meanwhile the Duke of Lorraine, who had been sick throughout the whole of the winter,

[2]A horsetail pennant used to lead the army.

and was not yet recovered from his sickness, could not immediately go to the army, and delayed this for more than a month,
which was the cause of much misfortune. While he was recovering his health, the Pasha of Neuhausel had time to strengthen his
fortress[3], and to prepare himself for defense.

The Governor of Grand, who also feared the Emperor's
forces gave similar orders to all those he commanded and arranged with the Pasha of Neuhausel to send him support if he
was attacked, or to receive it if Gran was attacked by the Christians.

This was the state of things when the Duke of Lorraine,
after having joined the army and reviewed it, in the presence of
the Emperor, the Duke of Bavaria and several other princes. He
then marched toward Gran and Neuhausel, without indicating
which place he would attack. When he was six leagues from both
of them he decided on a course of attack. He sent a detachment
of 6,000 horse forward, marched towards Grand, which caused
the Pasha of Neuhausel to think that was his target. To satisfy
the terms of his agreement with the Governor of Gran he sent
out 2,000 men from his garrison with orders to throw themselves
into Gran. However, as soon as the Duke of Lorraine knew that
they had entered Gran, he turned towards Neuhausel, which he
invested.

The Duke of Lorraine, delighted to see the garrison of
Neuhausel weakened, move quickly toward that city and after
having established his quarters, he summoned the Governor to
tell him that resistance would be in vain with only half the garrison he needed to hold his fortress. He would only have an hour
to make his decision, after which he would treat him, as one usually treats those who persist in an useless defense. The Pasha of
Neuhausel replied to the Duke of Lorraine that he did not know
what he meant, why he should not die at that very hour; that it
was the duty of those to defend the fortresses that the Great Lord
had given them. In fact, on the same day, he made a sortie against
our guard, which yielded to the ferocious attack of the Turks. The
alarm immediately spread through all our camp. The cavalry
mounted, and the Turks were repulsed. However, the Turks took
<u>many prisoners</u>, most of whom they beheaded.

[3]There was a star fort in the town that was considered one of the best forts of the era.

To further intimidate us they planted those heads on the walls of their city, which became a point of sadness for those who contemplated the deaths of their brothers, relatives or their friends, or at least their compatriots. This success inspired the Turks to make another sortie the next day, in which they took more prisoners that succumbed to the same fate as those of the previous day.

The Christians did not lack heart; while the sorties had stung them to do better in the future and at the cost of their vengeance, each competed to outdo the others. Our batteries were thus set up in a short time, the trench was opened, but there was never any hope of success, which we originally had, when a rumor was heard everywhere in the camp, that surprised many people. This rumor was that the Duke of Lorraine had complained loudly that Prince Hermann of Baden, the President of the War Council, who was in Vienna with the Emperor, prevented the things necessary for the siege to be sent to him, hoping by this means to destroy the Duke's reputation, and rendering himself more necessary. At length these rumors spread so far in the army, that

they reached the ears of Prince Louis of Baden, nephew of Herman, and he had some words with the Duke of Lorraine. Prince Herman was secretly jealousy of the Duke of Lorraine and was not sorry to see his enterprises run aground. Nevertheless, this encounter did not bode well for the Empire, but also of all the Christians alike. Many thought that this dispute was calmed down, if it was not extinguished.

Charles of Lorraine (17th century)

But it is well-known this thought was misplaced when one saw that of all the cannon shot sent to the Duke of Lorraine by Vienna, half of them were of the wrong caliber, which caused the cannon not to fire them properly.

Meanwhile, though the trenchworks continued to advance, the Duke of Lorraine received an order from the Emperor, signed by his own hand, by which he was ordered to raise the siege, and to throw forces into Raab, Commore, and Pressburg. No one could describe Lorraine's despair at this order, which he blamed on Prince Herman of Baden. However, being unable to disobey a direct order from the Emperor, he withdrew the posts nearest to the town, put his army into battle formation, and showed by his disposition that obedience was the only cause of his retreat. Finally, when the army started marching, he placed infantry in a few houses, which were about a quarter of a league away from the city, in the hope that, if he was followed, this infantry would protect his retreat, but also, that if the enemy appeared in front of this house, his infantry could take them in flank, and while they were shaken by the first discharge, the cavalry, which was in the rearguard, would turn against them, and defeat them easily.

One cannot say that the order was not given according to all the rules of war and that there had been all appearances that the siege would have succeeded. But the raising of the siege had so shaken the troops that when the Turks appeared the rearguard doubled its pace, instead of turning about, leaving those who had been posted in the houses without any hope of assistance. They defended themselves as best they could for an hour or two, but the location was indefensible, so this detachment surrendered and was taken prisoner.

This was not a happy arrangement for the prisoners for no sooner had the Pasha taken them back into Neuhausel than they were beheaded, and their heads placed on the ramparts with those who had died arms in hand. The Count of Taxis, who was from one of the best houses of Spain and whose ancestors had from time immemorial held the duty of the Grand Postmaster of this kingdom, was one of the unfortunate victims.[4]

The Christian army took the road to Schut Island and as it withdrew, they received word of a disaster greater than the lift-

---

[4]Anton Alexander (1662 – 1683)

ing of the siege of Neuhausel. This was the treason of the Hungarians who were at the crossing of the Vaag and who, instead of defending it, as expected, joined the forces of Count de Thököly, leader of the rebel Hungarians. They attacked the other troops, who were with them at the defense of the passage. I cannot relate how shocking this news was to the army. Everyone imagined they already had the Turks facing them, and thought only of avoiding them, but if they did not have arms and forces to oppose them, they would have ceded victory to the enemy without firing a shot. However, this augmentation of the Turkish forces

struck fear in everyone and of every party that was detached no more than half returned and generally in bad order. People too perverse pleasure in augmenting the forces of the enemy. Some said that that they had 300,000 men, others 400,000, and they exaggerated the cruelties that the Turks had committed along the road. It is true that one is ingenious when it comes to doing harm to oneself.

Imre Thököly, Prince of Transylvania (XVIIth century, unknown)

Finally, the Turks, after having crossed the Vaag, captured all the fortresses that were between that river and the Danube. By the time they reached that river, they constructed a bridge below Papa, over which they sent their infantry while the cavalry, with the baggage, crossed through Papa. However, as the army was very large, and these numbers in fact slowed them down. The Grand Vizier sent various detachments out, some [the Tartars] moving to pillage the region, others to pursue the Christian army,

which had not yet reached Schut Island. Those who were desig-
nated to pillage took a huge booty of all types. As the treachery of
the Hungarians had not been expected, everyone stayed in their
homes, thinking themselves far from the approaching danger.

After pillaging everything to satisfy their avarice, the Tartars gratified their cruelty with the blood of all the elderly. They
burned everything, sparing neither the houses of the princes nor
even the Emperor. Laxemburg was burned along with a large
number of castles, and soon knowledge of the Hungarian treachery reached Vienna. However, the Tartars, who had been employed in ruining so many men and so many beautiful buildings,
withdrew with the same speed with which they had come, fearing they might be cut off, again inflicting numerous cruelties on
anyone they encountered.

This news was soon known throughout our army spread
shock and consternation. The Duke of Lorraine could not find
anyone who was willing to get him news of the enemy. As soon
as he detached someone it was as if he'd sent him to his death,
so great was their strength and cruelty. The army continued
moving in three columns, the infantry in the lead, the cavalry
in the tail and the dragoons guarding the defiles. The baggage
was on the left and marched separately with the Savoy Dragoon
Regiment at the head under the Chevalier de Savoy, one of the
children of the Count de Soissons. The Taff Infantry Regiment
was also part of the baggage guard with a cavalry detached from
various units. As we came to the edge of a stream, a party that
the Duke of Lorraine had detached reported to him that the enemy were no more than a league away, which obliged him to
remain in the rearguard to give the orders should they encounter the enemy. But the fear was so great that instead of obeying
the command the cavalry abandoned the infantry and fled to the
protection of the cannons of Vienna. The Duke of Lorraine followed them to force their return to their post, but they refused to
listen, so he commanded the infantry to pass, in all diligence to
Schut Island, which was close and to entrench themselves. While
the vanguard passed, the Turks appeared and began to charge
the Montecuculli Regiment, which was with the rearguard. The
baggage was also attacked, and the Turks encountered so little
resistance that their victory was complete.

The Chevalier de Savoy, who was, as I have said, assigned the defense of the baggage had rallied some dragoons and some other men of good will who wished to oppose the fury of the Turks. However, these men were soon cut down and the Turks knocked the chevalier from his horse and his horse fell on top of him, the saddle horn piecing his stomach. The infantry fought behind the wagons and attempted to create a rampart against the blows of the Turks. The Turks, however, opened a passage, causing the Imperial troops to throw down their arms and flee, seeking to avoid a death that was very close and ignominious. The Turks finding them disarmed and defenseless simply cut them down without any risk to themselves.

Riamondo Montecuccoli (anonymous 17ᵗʰ century)

After killing eight hundred of our troops the Turks fell on the baggage, saving the rest of the army, which by this time had crossed to Schut Island. We lost 1,300 to 1,400 men in this battle among which were two princes, being the Chevalier de Savoy and the Prince d'Aremburg, three counts of the Empire, and several officers. In addition, the Turks captured a large quantity of baggage, the value of which was estimated at more than 300,000 écus. The Prince of Montecuculli alone lost 20,000 écus. Prince Louis of Baden lost a considerable sum and the other officers lost sums in proportion to their means.

But no matter how much they felt their loss, there were nevertheless many other things in their heads, which were far more embarrassing. The infantry saw itself abandoned by the cavalry and did not know what would happen. The Duke of Lorraine had gone after the cavalry, and word was impatiently awaited from him. He wasted no time, and was resolved to die, or to disengage his infantry. In fact, after having made some reproaches to the cavalry, he told them that to repair their fault they must to return to the enemy; that it had only to follow him, and that he hoped with the grace of God, whatever difficulty there was in his enterprise, it would be quickly overcome.

The Turks, anticipating his plan, moved before him to dispute his passage, but the Duke of Lorraine threw himself first in to the middle of the enemy fire, opened the passage, saber in hand, after having cut down those who sought to oppose him. Finally, he rejoined his infantry, with extraordinary joy. They expressed their joy at having been saved from peril, but as the main body of the Ottoman army approached, he threw part of his infantry into Raab, Commore, and Pressburg, then retreated with the rest and with his cavalry to Vienna.

The Emperor, who was seriously alarmed by the sudden invasion of the Turks, and who considered that after the betrayal of the Hungarians, he could no longer remain in security in Vienna, thought of leaving. But before leaving he increased the privileges of the students, who were already very great and very considerable, in order that they should receive compensation for the courage they had shown against Suleiman until the city was besieged; this was an encouragement for them to defend it with the same firmness. He also granted the right of control to all the shoemaker apprentices, who numbered about 1,500 in order to take up arms in protection of the land. Finally, after giving control of the city to Starhemberg, who he made its governor, this prince was obliged to go and take with him all that was most precious to him. The Emperor took the road to Linz, accompanied by the two empresses, his children, ministers, and the other numerous members of the Austrian Court.

Everyone wept at his departure, and it was unbelievable to many that this prince should not weep himself. He could not believe that he was being forced to abandon his people to the mercy of the infidels. Meanwhile everyone hastened to follow him, so as to not experience the misfortunes which were anticipated. Finally, as there were not sufficient carriages to take away all those who wanted to leave, many women of quality went up to the palace footmen, so that one saw the first prince of the world, followed by all the flower of the nobility of Germany, go as if in exile amid the tears and the groans of all his people, who presented themselves in his path, all melting into tears. Some of the Jesuits, who were delighted to follow the Emperor for several reasons, climbed into a carriage, and the people turned their compassion on seeing them into a frightful rage. Since they knew that their lust for the goods of another was the cause of all these misfortunes, they threw themselves upon them, and very few escaped his vengeance.

The Emperor, however, marched with a glum face, and accepted his fate. The others kept in a sad silence, and though everyone had to abandon their things, no one knew if they were more touched by their own misfortune than that of the Emperor. Finally, this march assumed a funeral like pallor augmented further by more sadness and compassion. The far bank of the Danube was in flames. The Emperor stopped his carriage not initially knowing what it was, but soon realized it was the Turks who were giving further evidence of their cruelty. He could not hold back his tears, but did everything possible to conceal his sadness, but never mastered it.

Once he arrived in Linz, he waited there for several days for the court the to gather, as they had not been able to leave at the same time as he. And once everyone went near his person he left for Passau, where he had resolved to await his fate. Everyday news came to him which beat him down completely. He learned that all of Hungary, had risen up against him, and that he had to defy the leaders of this country, who were with his staff and who began to act against his interests. Meanwhile the Turkish army was still advancing towards Vienna, which obliged the Duke of Lorraine, who could not resist it, to pull everyone into the fortress, and to retire to that side of the Danube. He brought in 12,000 men, who were joined the garrison, which was 3,000 men, giving the city a total of 15,000 men, not counting the students, the craftsmen, and the other inhabitants capable of service.

Emperor Leopold I, HRE 1640-1705 (Benjamin von Block)

Seeing that the Turks were marching directly on Vienna, Starhemberg gathered all the people and spoke to them, the substance of which was that before the enemy closed the roads, he wished to know those who wished to leave the city and those who wished to remain; that they had only to say freely, because he would not wish more for one than for the others; and that, indeed, he meant to say to those who were determined to remain with him, that he would to defend himself to the utmost, so that if they did not feel brave enough to share with him the glory, and the peril, which were to accompany all their actions, it would be better to be leave than to remain. At these words everyone cried out that he was ready to die for his country, and Starhemberg seeing their goodwill, asked them to raise their hands, to show that they would be faithful to God and the Emperor. At the same time an infinite number of hands were seen in the air, each pushing cries to Heaven as a sign of fidelity.

Giving them permission to leave, Starhemberg sent the useless mouths out of the city, such as the elderly and those not fit for service. But having wished to send the women out, they begged him not to do it and promised to work as hard as the soldiers, which they did, so only a small number left. He also had an inventory made of all war material and food, finding much more than he thought he needed, but very few cattle for such a large garrison. He also found there was little gunpowder and other war material, and he did not know who to hold accountable, because there had been more than sufficient time to accumulate sufficient quantities of everything. All that one could say was that one hoped the city would be relieved before the supplies ran out. Otherwise, one could only blame the negligence of the ministers, who had thought that the Turks would not dare to start their campaign there and were content to provide sufficient provisions for Raab, Commore, and Pressburg, which they thought to be the most exposed. However, this is not an excuse for them, as they should have anticipated this before it occurred.

Without wishing to take up personal matters here, I will only say that the Turks, finding no one else in the countryside to resist them, spread out their army in such a way that it covered more than ten leagues in front. They thus burned a great deal of the country, and after having left marks of their cruelty, the army attacked the islands on the Danube, near Vienna, and having taken possession of them, they cut the communications with the city.

On the other side, the detachments that the Grand Vizier had sent out had taken many castles, burning those that were useless to them, and put garrisons in the others to protect their convoys. They had left many troops around Raab, Commore, and Pressburg to hold the garrisons in place so they could not trouble their foragers and prevent those which daily sought to rejoin the Christian army, but the way was not safe. Thököly[5], who had stirred up trouble in Hungary, where he had contacts with all the great men, and many of whom were his relatives had, however, moved to the Polish frontier to prevent not only the enforcement of an alliance, of which I will speak later, which had been concluded between the Emperor and the King of Poland, but also to capture several castles that were favorable to this plan. He took several without firing a shot, because the great men of

the region, sought any pretext to take up arms against the Empire. They were quite ready to serve Thököly and did not fail to publish that they could not do otherwise than declare for the strongest side, since they had been abandoned by those who was to protect them. They joined their troop such that they were daily considerably reinforced. There was only baron of the region, named Johannelli, who fought to defend his castle at Panowitz and who obliged Thököly to attack him in a regular siege.

Ernst Rüdiger Graf von Starhemberg, 1638-1701 (Peter Schenk)

As he was situated on the summit of a mountain and it was difficult to carry cannon up it to attack him, he kept Thököly longer than he had desired for the good of his affairs. While he was occupied before Panowitz Castle, General Schuts, who had orders to join the troops of the Prince Lubomirski[6], who was advancing from Poland in great diligence, hastened to execute his

[5]Imre Thököly (1657 – 1705)
[6]Hieronim Augustyn Lubomirski (1648 – 1706)

orders, before Thököly could block him. As a result, Thököly found himself missing an opportunity and responded by attacking Panowitz Castle that his cannon had made a breach wide enough for ten men to march abreast. Resolved to assault, Baron Johannelli, whose garrison consisted of 200 men, plus people who had saved their goods and sought refuge in the castle, he sent Thököly an offer of conditions for his surrender. But, Thököly was so angry, as I have just said, because he had lost time that he could have used more usefully elsewhere, that he would only accept unconditional surrender. Some Hungarian lords who were his relatives, as well as those of Johannelli, intervened to save Johannelli's life.

Thököly encamped at Tokay, where, having learned that the Grand Vizier was marching towards Eseg, he set out with 2,000 cavalrymen, and to confer with him on what he had to do during the campaign. The reception which the Grand Vizier gave Thököly surprised those who accompanied him, which was accompanied by testimonies of admiration and confidence. But this minister had his views on doing this, considering that it was necessary to ingratiate the Hungarian lords who were there, that he had come to assist them rather than to increase the states of the Great Lord, which were already too large and too vast. He received him, therefore, not as a baron of the country, but as one to whom his master had reserved the Crown of Hungary, of which he was very glad to give him assurances, in the presence of the principal Turks and Hungarians. As a result, this news spread everywhere and produced the effect he expected of it. He ordered him, however, to occupy the pass at Oralva, which he believed that the King of Poland would use to come west, assuring him that it was on this that the success of the promises he made to him in the name of the Great Lord depended.

This was the state of affairs when the Grand Vizier arrived before Vienna. Initially he attacked the Leopoldstadt Suburb, which was separated from the city by a branch of the Danube and gained control of it after a relentless combat. He then constructed two bridges over the river to have communications with all his troops, which were separated here and there, some on the islands and others on the mainland. However, he was still awaiting the arrival of his heavy cannon, but they did not arrive quickly because, as I have said earlier, he could not move up the Danube because of the fortresses held by the Imperials which forced him to bring them overland by roads that were difficult and broken. So as to not to lose any time, the Grand Vizier had lines of trench-works constructed that were very irregular because of the nature of the ground, though they were no less strong because of that. They were cannon proof, secured by good forts, and by good re-doubts, which were constructed at intervals.

Until the lines of circumvallation were completed, a third of the Ottoman army was always in bivouac and the rest retired into their tents where they were ordered to always hold them-selves ready for the first command, such that their horses were saddled all night. When the lines were completed, they were only guarded by a detachment, which allowed other parts of the army some rest, as it was greatly fatigued from the work of construct-ing the lines. For it was not only obliged to watch for one day in three, as I have said, but they had to remain on horseback, or to work on making fascines. We had, however, made a great mis-take on our side, for instead of ruining the country, and harvest-ing the wheat, to inconvenience the enemy, both were kept with great care. Because of this their army, as numerous as it was in cavalry, never had far to go to find forage.

While all this was occurring, Count von Starhemberg at-tempted to disrupt their work on the lines of circumvallation with frequent sorties. However, rather being placed in an ad-vantageous, his men faced such a great multitude of Turks, that he was always obliged to flee, contenting himself to firing his cannon, which inflicted casualties on the Turks and forced them to take cover. Once the lines were completed and the trench was traced out, they worked on opening it and 4,000 horses were placed behind an epaulement to support the workers. The can-non fire from the city was extraordinary during all the night and Count von Starhemberg had many illuminating artifices fired to better discover on what side the Turks were working.

Once the Turkish heavy cannon had arrived, they were placed on small hills, which had been picked out earlier, in order that they might have the best effect. The Grand Vizier placed 20,000 of his best troops around these batteries to defend them in case the Christians attempted to spike the guns. An Italian, who had gone into the Turkish camp, had assured them that this was Count von Starhemberg's plan. Though the enterprise seemed so difficult to him, such as he could scarcely believe it, he was always glad to have nothing to reproach himself with and took all precautions. He had four batteries constructed, two of which would be on one bastion, so that one could say that it was the same, except that they ruined it on two sides. For the other two, they fired on two other works, and all these works defended the town on the side of the Scottish Gate and the Red Gate, by which the Grand Vizier had intended to attack the city.

When the batteries were ready to fire, they were well served. The first day they fired 1,000 rounds and on the second and third 1,600 each. All the artillery of the city was dismounted on those days an\d many were wounded including several officers. This shelling threw great fear into the city, which was further augmented by the heated shot that set fires in many locations and were very difficult to extinguish. The bourgeois, who were not at all accustomed to these disasters, had already lost much of their firmness of heart. Count von Starhemberg knew that there was already talk of surrender in the city, so he had gallows erected in the market, swearing in front of a gathering of the principal citizens, that he would hang the first of them that dared to speak of surrender.

This threat drove the most fearful back to their duty and obedience. However, he feared that the bourgeois would spread their fear to the soldiers, so he prevented the soldiers from having any communication with them. Though he had originally thought to distribute some of them among the companies of the militia, to teach them the proper technique for fighting, he changed his mind out of concern, as I have said, that their fear would infect the others.

The Emperor, was in Passau as I have said earlier, received couriers daily from the Duke of Lorraine, who sent him what he needed to know about the siege, even though he was very ill-informed himself. Two men that Starhemberg had sent him had been taken by the Turks, as they attempted to pass through their camp, and had been immediately hung, because the count's letters had been found. He could therefore only know what experience had taught him, which took pleasure in imaging things worse than they were, each one regulating the present events, on the past events, which had not been very happy. The Emperor was in mortal fear of what he was about to face. For, on the other hand, the King of France, after marching his troops towards the frontier of Germany, went there himself, and it was reported that he was marching against Cologne, or against Philipsburg, having contacts in these two fortresses. As a matter of fact, in the latter fortress a certain Nigrelly was suspected of being in his pay, and in the other fortress there was great suspicion, knowing that he was responsible for all those bloody tragedies that had been committed there for some time. The King of Spain, moreover, was dangerously ill, and as no one hoped for his health any more, the Emperor considered that, if he died, it would be a pretext for the King of France, who would have claims disentangle with him and would throw himself on the Empire, which he could not attack, out of fear of becoming subject to the scorn of the Christian princes.

Though he was occupied by all sorts of fears, there were two bits of good news, one that the King of France had returned to Paris and the other that the King of Spain was recovering. All that remained to be heard was that the siege of Vienna was going badly for the Grand Vizier, but instead he learned that daily the Turks reinforced their army, daily came out of their camp, and that their works continued advancing. This evil news banished the joy from his heart resulting from the other two bits of news. The Emperor forgot nothing of what had to be done. Daily he sent couriers to all the courts to press them to send assistance and to entreat the princes to promptly march.

It was via the Marquis de Seppeville, Envoy of the King of France to the Emperor, that the bad news of what had happened in the siege was received, rather than by any better source. He had taken great care, which made it suspect to the Emperor, to deliver it to all the court and to the King, his master, to whom he sent four couriers in a week. He hoped, perhaps, to give him much joy, but at the same time he inspired the desires of the Prince of Conti, who was also displeased, that the King had given his Duke of Maine his son the Government of Languedoc, who had been promised the hand of Mademoiselle de Blois in marriage, to go and distinguish himself in fighting against the Turks. He communicated his plan only to Prince Eugene of Savoy, brother of the Chevalier de Savoy, who had been killed in the service of the Emperor, as I have said above, lest by communicating it to more than one-person word of his plan might reach the King's ears.

He resolved to leave the French court on Monday, 25 July, and having commanded his coach driver to wait at the Royal Palace, where the Duke d'Orléans had come from Versailles. He mounted his horse with Prince Eugene, followed only by a page and without his colors, and took the road to Senlis. Two posts from this city, that is to say, between Senlis and Paris, a postilion recognized him, such that the Prince de Conti spoke to him, and the other responded. The Prince de Conti asked him if he knew him and the other said yes, so he gave him four pistoles, so that he would not tell anyone he had gone that way, switched hats with the postilion, thinking that this would prevent him from being so easily recognized. The postilion, however, had no sooner left him than he took the hat to the country house of de Condé, who gave it to Gourville, the intendant of the Prince de Condé, who was the uncle of the Prince de Conti.

We were extremely anxious as to of what had become of him, for his coachman who had been waiting for him at the Royal Palace until 11:00 pm, which had put his whole house in alarm. And as it was well-known that he had left the court, it put the Princess de Conti in pain, but not so much as the King, who could not imagine what had become of him. The King had sent word of this bad news to the Prince de Condé, who was then at Paris, by the Duke de la Feuillade, and this prince, who was ready to return to Chantilly, had gone to serve as a pledge of the fidelity of his nephew. Meanwhile, those who thought they knew him, said that he was not at all unhappy with this disappearance, which showed that the Prince de Conti had courage, and that he could not suffer the Duke de Maine, without showing any resentment.

When the court was certain of the route he had taken, the King dispatched several couriers to wait for him along the road and gave to one of them, named Saintrailles, who was going to the Prince de Condé, a letter for him, written in his own hand, in which he called him "my son," but at the same time warned that if he did not return immediately, he never wished to see him again. However, as after all this was done, there was great uncertainty, if he would obey or not, the Prince de Condé sent him a letter of credit of 20,000 écus, knowing that he had only taken 600 pistoles with him, and that he would need it if he went further. But, as this would make him want to continue his journey sooner than to break it, everyone was of the opinion that the Prince de Condé would be kind enough not to show himself so obedient.

The departure of this prince, to go and distinguish himself by fighting the Turks, now that there was no doubt where he had gone, was the subject of conversation of many people, some of whom attributed this resolution to the reason I mentioned above while others attributed it to unhappiness with his marriage.

Returning to Saintrailles however, he arrived at Brussels the same day that he had left Versailles. Knowing that the Prince de Conti had only passed by there and that he had taken the road to Cologne, he went to Namur, where he went down the Meuse to Liege, to go from there. Then taking up post horses at Liege, he acted diligently and reached the Prince de Conti, showing him the King's letter, the threats that he had made, and asked him to obey. The prince embraced the Prince of Savoy, of whom the King had made no mention, and who was resolved to continue his voyage. The Prince de Conti gave Prince Eugene a diamond of great value, and returned to France by short trips, letting Saintrailles precede him, to report to the King. Saintrailles found the King greatly distressed by the death of the queen, which had occurred two or three days before; that he had not had time to think of the Prince de Conti. Nevertheless, it was good to know that he was doing his duty, which was important to him, considering he had plans for meditating the war, because while he sought to ruin the House of Austria, that Austria had a prince of blood in its hands, from whom it could hope for a big ransom, supposing that Austria could not cause him to take up arms against his duty to France.

The affairs of the Prince of Conti, having some relation to the subject I am dealing with here, as I have caused the reader to judge, and having been unable to dispense of speaking about it, I shall now return to the siege of Vienna, which the Turks continued with success, but sometimes contrary. Count von Starhemberg, seeing that they were advancing their labors, continued to attempt a few sorties, in one of which he had so well led them, that if all their cavalry had not come to their assistance with the Janissaries, he could have hoped to fill the trench, having made this plan to support his people by many pioneers, and by other workers. But the Turks now outnumbered him; he caused the retreat to be sounded, and, which he did in good order, losing none of the good officers or soldiers.

Louis XVI, 1661 (Charles Le Brun)

He discovered a dangerous undertaking which two Christians had made over the city, one of which was Albanian and the other from Candia [Greece]. They attempted to set fire to it, claiming to extinguish a fire started by a heated shot, but instead of water, they were found with straw in hand; they were arrested and put to the question, where they confessed their crime. They were united in the final punishment. Their heads were cut off and placed on the wall not only to warn the Turks, that their plans had been discovered, but also to return to duty those who might also take such a resolution.

The Ottoman army, however, being unable to receive provisions, except by means of camels and wagons, food was not abundant and was often lacking. Forage for the horses, moreover, began to become scarce around the army, and they had to go farther. In this necessity the Grand Vizier sent part of his cavalry to the side of the Raab and brought into his camp a part of the infantry, which was on that side, which he needed more than cavalry. With this infantry, which was all fresh, the work advanced greatly. And the Grand Vizier, seeing himself no farther from the counterscarp than ten paces at most, resolved to attack it, after he had detonated a mine, on the ruins of which he believed he would be easier to make a lodgment. The mine blew up on the side of the besiegers, and many who had advanced to be ready to mount the assault were buried. The Grand Vizier these troops were quickly replaced by others, the counterscarp was attacked with such vigor, that it was taken at sword point. But Starhemberg, who considered that if he gave the Turks time to establish a lodgment there would mean the loss of the city, launched a counterattack with fresh men, who, after a great battle, fought on both sides, drove the Turks out, after making a great slaughter of them.

The Turks seeking to regain their honor and retake the counterscarp detonated another mine which had more effect than the previous. It blew part of the work into the air with some men on it. This so intimidated the Christians that many fled, while the Janissaries, supported by workers, carried the counterscarp. At the same time they entrenched themselves, but Count von Starhemberg, who had run to the scene, launched an attack against their works, sword in hand, and having mixed a number of grenadiers, in whom he had great confidence, with his soldiers, the Janissaries, who did not have time to take cover, still received the attackers bravely. The Turks, having advanced their grenadiers, as they had the advantage of height over the Christians, took a heavy toll on them. Von Starhemberg seeing that they were folding, called the retreat when he saw his efforts were useless. However, as he had countermined the counterscarp from the side of the city and his mine had not been disturbed, as soon as his troops were under cover in the bastion, he had his mine detonated. It threw many Turks into the air, some of which fell among their own men, who were crushed. The Turks were in great disorder and Starhemberg sought to profit from this, returning at the charge and not giving them time to reorganize. A battalion then came to their support and the battle resumed with great violence, but with a very different outcome. The Turks, seeing themselves reinforced, instead of losing courage, pushed back while the Christians began to fold again. They had before their eyes a terrible spectacle that would shake the most resolved and they could not take a step without passing over the bodies of their companions, most of whom, half dead, were trampled to death by the fleeing multitude.

Seeing his plan to retake the counterscarp had failed and being unable to re-establish order among his troops, Starhemberg abandoned retaking it and sought to retain what had escaped the Turkish attack. After retreating and taking care of the wounded, he reviewed what remained of his troops. He found that they had been reduced by a third, not only by dead, wounded, and prisoners, but by others who were returning into the city. The effect of fatigue combined with the poor food had so weakened them that they fell sick daily. Many of the sick were unable to man the walls or work. Even Starhemberg found himself sick and as the city feared it could not defend itself without him, he was asked to rest and recover, while the principal officers who were still healthy offered to take care of his duties. Starhemberg, however, considered quite properly, that in the state of affairs in the city, he should set the example of duty and continue as if he were in full health.

Meanwhile the Turks, after having made themselves masters of the counterscarp, and having repaired it as best they could, in order to preserve it, lodged cannon in it, which began to cause great disorder in the city. They knocked down more than 30 feet of the wall, with part of the ravelin.[7] Starhemberg, intending to remedy it, had an entrenchment dug in the city opposite the wall which the Turks had ruined. As for the ravelin, he wanted to have it repaired, but the cannon of the enemy prevented it, and he was obliged to content himself with having it half-repaired.

The Duke of Lorraine had placed his camp between Vienna and Krems, beyond the Danube, where he had a boat (pontoon) bridge, over which he passed all his troops. He protected the bridgehead with two good forts, where he had positioned cannon, and infantry, so that the enemy, who wished to dislodge him, sent a detachment to surprise Tulm, which would have ren-

---

[7]A triangular fortification or detached emplacement, sometimes called a demi-lune outside a castle or in front of the curtain wall.

dered his bridge ineffective. This would have made them masters of the city. Once they had thrown a garrison into it, the Duke's parties could not reach beyond the Danube, as they had done before. The Duke of Lorraine having heard of this plan, sent word to Tulm to be careful not to be surprised. However, in order not to let the enemy return without a fight, he organized a detachment on his side, about the same strength of the enemy, and once these forces meet, they surprised each other so completely, that a large number were killed. The advantage was, however, on the side of the Christians, who put the Turks to rout. They did not dare pursue them for long, for fear of falling into some ambush, so they were obliged to content themselves with what they had won, and to have caused the Turkish plan to fail.

This success was followed by others. Two or three Christian units engaged the Turks, killing a large part of them and taking the rest prisoners of war. As these engagements were not decisive and without proper relief, Vienna was in great danger. Messages were sent to every court, which had previously promised to send troops promptly. The Pope not only joined his priests to those of the Emperor, but in many letters, by which he granted indulgences to all those who sent money to help Vienna and assured going to Paradise for those who died, weapons in hand, to support this just cause. As he knew well, however, all this would have little effect if it was not joined by effective relief, he sent great sums to the Emperor, of which part came from him and the other cardinals, who did it as much out of devotion as to assure their fortunes, which would be in great danger if Vienna succumbed. The Pope also sent Ranucci to France in the capacity of a nuncio, bearing a letter to the King of France asking him to contribute to the delivery of Vienna. In order for him to be better received, he gave him the relics of Jesus' swaddling clothes to present them to the Duke of Burgundy, son of the Dauphin. But as the King found that he was aware of it a little late, he sent orders to Ranucci not to pass Orléans, under the pretext of the journey he was about to make to the frontier, since what I have related occurred in May.

Dysentery spread through the city to the point where about one hundred people died of it every day. It cut down the bourgeois and the soldiers equally. As for Starhemberg, if the good food he had, and the others did not have, on one side helped him recover, God who did not want to forsake the Christians by the loss of Vienna, permitted his health to be gradually re-established, in order that he might continue his duty, as he had already begun. Nevertheless, things in the city continued to decline. On one hand the garrison was on its knees, and on the other the assistance, though coming, people in the pay of France spread rumors to the King of Poland, who tried to insinuate that his kingdom would be in danger if he took his forces away, while dangerous enemies were at the door, and capable of taking advantage of his absence. Nevertheless, they received news of him from time to time, by which he sent word that he was going to march incessantly, these insensibilities balanced the contrary opinions, which Starhemberg took great care to conceal from his garrison, because he feared that such wicked news would negatively affect the morale of his soldiers, who had appeared too already affected by their misfortunes, and by the dangerous malady with which they were afflicted.

The disease that afflicted the city was further affected by the stench of the unburied rotting bodies, which was as dangerous as in the time of the plague. This caused many issues in the city, because Starhemberg did not wish to accord a truce to the Grand Vizier to recover the bodies of those who had been killed in the various attacks, hoping that, in addition to the inconvenience which he would suffer, it would still produce a spectacle which offered courage to these soldiers, who, in marching to their enterprises, would see before their eyes the fate of their companions. Be that as it may be, whether it was this infection or something else which attracted them to the different things in the city, it was so inconvenient, that they wished to be delivered from the enemies before them. This disease, however, also reigned in the camp of the Turks, where more than three hundred died every day, but of which they were hardly aware, because they received new forces, which repaired their losses. As they were not accustomed to the fatigue, most fell sick after two days, which increased their confusion rather than their confidence.

Starhemberg, who had news of everything that happened in their camp, took upon himself the task of encouraging his people to patience, saying that the coming of the King of Poland would complete the ruin of the Turks, and the deliverance of the city. However, now was the time for him to come. The Turks, having been advised that he had actually set out, made new efforts to make themselves masters of the city every day. They had captured a bastion, surpassing themselves, if we may so speak. Whatever the Christians might have done with heroic resistance, and such as could be expected of people animated by a noble despair, all this had served only to further exploit the valor of their enemies. The bastion was taken, and they then attacked a ravelin, of which I have spoken, with whose capture they continued to show their courage, and compelled all who were within it to abandon it. But a mine which the Christians made, having blown up at the same time, they found another kind of death; the death which they had despised under another circumstance.

They then attempted cross the moat, raising their gabions and their galleries, and pounding the city more than ever with cannon, preparing to carry it by a general assault, before the King of Poland could arrive. The day was chosen for so great a purpose on 29 August, a sacred day among them, which they solemnized with great superstition. Meanwhile the Grand Vizier encouraged his officers, pushing them more, telling them that the day had come to finish their labors and he exhorted them to inspire their soldiers. To satisfy the command of the Vizier, these officers assembled their men and stood at the head of each of their regiments, under the pretext of inspecting their arms. As they were talking about the enterprise which the Grand Vizier had ordered, they told their men that it was all they needed to do to put an end to the war in a single day. If they took Vienna, not only would all the Christian fortresses, which were in Hungary, surrender, without the necessity of firing a single shot. In turn this would open Germany up to them, where there were strong fortresses, but which was a good and fertile land, where everyone would find the reward of his labors. As they spoke to them, the Grand Vizier, who had come out of his tent, to authorize by his presence the exhortations of the captains, appeared from one end of the line to the other, where, in passing, he smiled at each, to show them that he approved of what the captains had said.

He then carefully arranged all the things necessary for the attack. Although Starhemberg was extremely apprehensive that day, he gave his orders to recall his forces on such an urgent occasion. He had burned the gallery that the Turks had made in the moat, having thrown several incendiaries on the fascines, with which they began to fill the moat, and started them burning, even though the Turks had rushed to the moat to extinguish them. To those in the city the fire was so great in this encounter, that no one had seen the like, and as the Turks were trying to extinguish the fire there were several killed, and many wounded.

This success raised the hearts of the Christians, but did not lower that of the Turks, who, as if by a prelude, were preparing for their general assault, and tried to force the Christians by several attempts, sometimes seeming to want to carry the city. And although they did not use all their strength, they did not leave the garrison so fatigued, even though their weariness grew day by day.

It was at this time that the Grand Vizier claimed he would make himself master of the city that he allowed Count Capara, who had been held back under various pretexts, to return to the Emperor. As this circumstance may serve to portray those who imagine, this Empire has an end in politics and power, I will say here, under what pretext he was detained, and this was nevertheless the true cause of his detention.

As the Sultan had learned that the Christians were only joining together because of the distress of the Emperor, he always entertained the thought of amusing them with a few propositions of peace. But Capara, seeing that it was folly to stop there, seeing that he was asking for no less than the Crown of Hungary, had wanted to leave several times without being allowed to. The affair of Count Serin, who the Emperor had arrested, on account of his contacts with Thököly, gave a pretext to the Sultan, who did not know how to retain this minister; he then agreed to serve as a hostage until he knew how Count Serin was treated, and that the Emperor had granted him his protection. All this proceeded, however, only to have a person near him, to whom he could make proposals for peace, in the case that the King of Poland, together with the other Christian princes, would proceed to the assistance of Vienna. However, since this prince was still very far away, and that he would have taken the city before he could come to its aid, the Grand Vizier dismissed Capara, who was delighted that he had taken this resolution, being held too long in the hands of a barbarous prince, whose will served as law to those who were under his power. This was the state of things when Count von Starhemberg had found the means, by paying a bounty, to send news to the Duke of Lorraine, telling him that relief was necessary. He told him that the garrison was greatly weakened and though it showed the same resolution, he was afraid, nonetheless, that its force would weaken before its courage. He informed him that gunpowder and grenades would soon be lacking, though he thought for the moment that he had a sufficient amount, if it was true, as was said, that the King of Poland would soon arrive. The Duke of Lorraine wrote back using the same messenger. The messenger succeeded in getting back into Vienna without mishap and he had no sooner given Starhemberg the dispatch than the Governor saw that they confirmed the arrival of the King of Poland and that the city would soon be relieved. He immediately sent this word to the inhabitants and the garrison.

Everyone was encouraged by this news and resolved to hold out and resist the Turks when they finally launched their general assault. The hope of soon being delivered from peril made them not only look upon what they had already experienced, as a matter of little consequence, but they had disdain for those that still threatened them. Members of the bourgeois asked to serve as guards in place of the soldiers, whom they wished to relieve from this for other concerns, but though Starhemberg did not doubt of their goodwill, he would not entrust to them posts of consequence, afraid that if the enemy appeared they would not be as firm as the soldiers, whom he had repeatedly seen show more resolve.

At last, on that great day, when the Turks were to perform so many marvels, they came under arms to the sound of all their drums, all their musicians[8], and all their trumpets. They made several maneuvers to display all of their forces so as to create more terror. And after making several countermarches, the cannon, which had fired from the daybreak, with more noise than effect, suddenly ceased, until a general discharge was fired, which

---

[8]Translator: The word used was "hautbois" which generally means "oboe," but when used in a military context means "musicians." I suspect, however, in this case the author is generally talking about all instruments other than percussion or brass.

was the signal for the assault.

At the same time, the defenders saw the Turks, who all fought together in the trench, were ordered to march in separated directions; some were armed with axes, others with offensive weapons, but all with much pride. The assault lasted six hours, during which the Christians suffered greatly. As the Turks constantly refilled their ranks, as soon as the Christians cut down one enemy, a second took his place, and when they cut him down a third stepped forward, unconcerned of the fate of his two predecessors. The town burghers, whom the Earl of Starhemberg had put under arms, some to guard the public squares, others to guard the avenues, knowing that all their fortune depended on the defense presented by the soldiers, asked Count von Starhemberg if they could help them. Starhemberg, who saw his men were ready to succumb under the Turkish numbers, was delighted that they were in that mood. And making them remember that their wives, their children, their freedom, and their religion depended on the defense, he animated them so much that they presented themselves on the breach with more confidence than he believed they had. The combat, which seemed to have slackened because of the fatigue of the soldiers, began again with great fury. The Turks, who had promised themselves a sure victory, despaired of seeing it snatched from their hands, and fought on in despair. But the Christians, having no less reason than to fight for their lives, repelled them so vigorously, and helped by the soldiers who had regained their courage, and by the advantage which the besieged exerted on the besiegers, they forced the Turks to turn their backs, even though a great number remained on the breach. The Grand Vizier, seeing that several places had been going bad for him in the battle, sounded the retreat fearing that things might go from bad to worse. He withdrew to his camp out of sadness and despair. After this effort, he had lost more than 5,000 men, not counting the wounded, who were almost equal in number. He feared, not without reason, that his troops might mutiny against him. The Janissaries had suffered greatly in all these attacks, and in particular the last one. They now demanded that the siege be raised immediately, adding that of the 12,000 of them that had been there six weeks earlier, there was now no more than half of them who were in a condition to fight.

This beginning sedition further angered the Grand Vizier, who had been started by the failure of the attack and to stifle it in the cradle he used the Aga[9], the man who commanded them, and obtained from him by his intervention, that they would return to duty in return for a sum of money. This was the method normally used to appease their discontent, but instead of being useful on this occasion, the problems reoccurred.

Janissaries circa 1683 (Knötel)

---

[9]Aga or Agha is an military title used for the head of a corps.

The Grand Vizier was no sooner out of this trouble, then another appeared. He learned that the King of Poland, after having deceived Tekely's vigilance, was on his way to the assistance of Vienna by forced marches. He learned that the Polish vanguard had already arrived on the banks of the Danube and that the King would join them in a few days. At this news he caused his wounded and sick to be transported out of his camp, and after having added new defensive works to it, he thought of reducing the town before the Poles came to attack him, which was not yet possible for a few days, their army being fatigued by a long march and in need of rest.

A number of princes had personally joined, the Emperor's army with their troops, such as the Duke of Bavaria and the Duke of Saxony. In addition to them men came from all parts of Christianity, with the exception of France, who had not permitted a large number of the most qualified lots to go. These forces were sufficient to raise the siege of Vienna without waiting for the King of Poland, supposing that it took him too long to come. But as the two dukes did not wish to obey the Duke of Lorraine, nor would the Duke of Lorraine surrender command to them, all these forces were useless until the King of Poland arrived to bring them into accord.

As for the Marquis of Brandenburg, he had flattered the Emperor for some time about sending him considerable help. While he was in a hurry to execute what he had promised, he was stopped by his alliance with France, which he had not been able to use in this way; he then sought a pretext to recant, for which he demanded the Duchies of Brieg, Lignitz, and Wolnaw in exchange, upon which he claimed to have a legitimate right. Certainly, the Emperor was reduced to such a great extremity that it was believed that he would rather grant these demands than deprive himself of his help. But as the Marquis of Brandenburg made these demands, as I have just said, only to have a pretext to get out of his engagement, he added another request, that he knew very well that the Emperor would not grant him. He asked for the freedom of conscience for the Protestants of Silesia, which caused the Emperor to understand the Marquis' demands and no longer expected his promises.

The Count of Waldeck, who had been declared a prince of the Empire not long before, and who had been given command of the troops of the Circles, also joined the Emperor's army. Because of his experience at war and his zeal for service he thought he too should be consulted on the way to save Vienna. The Emperor approved all that the count had said on this, but he waited for the arrival of the King of Poland before taking a final decision, and this advice and all the other that he had received on the same subject, only pleased him at the moment, and all order was changed once this prince had arrived.

Kara Mustapha (anonymous)

On 2 September, the King of Poland arrived at Holbron, with his most magnificent cavalry, but it was fatigued. The Duke of Lorraine, who had taken care to organize magazines, in order that the army of this prince could recover in a few days, found him in Holbron, where the King of Poland received him with great expressions of friendship and confidence, even though they had been rivals in the pursuit of the Polish Crown. The Duke of

Bavaria and the Duke of Saxony went there also to greet the King of Poland who presented his son, Alexander, to them. The Prince was 17-18 years old and had come to experience war for the first time, under the King, his father, who could give him good lessons. The first greetings completed, they held a council of war, not to know if they could relieve Vienna, because that had long been resolved, but to determine how they would go about it.

These nobles resolved it amongst themselves and communicated it to the Emperor, who approved it. Now there was no further question to prepare the necessary things for such a great plan and as the countryside was not only ruined and the houses were uninhabitable, such that one could not hope for the least thing, it was necessary to move with faith and the provisions for the troops and forage for the horses.

The Grand Vizier knew of the great preparations that the Christians had made against him and prepared to defend himself. However, he didn't do this without some concern on his part. He spoke with his principal officers, who were of the opinion that they should withdraw to the Neuhausel, alleging that the army was greatly fatigued by this long and unsuccessful siege, that the soldiers needed rest; that most of them had never seen any other combat, other than that which had presented itself during the siege. How could they resist an army, which was composed of the flower of all Christianity, and where there was such a great number of the most qualified princes and nobility, who had come there only to conquer, or to die? There was no reason to expose the remains of an unfortunate army against a refreshed army, and against a garrison that had shown its valor by the defeat of their best troops. They argued that while there was still time, it was necessary to save not only the army, but also the reputation of the Grand Vizier, which was already wounded by so unfruitful a siege, and where he had lost more than 30,000 men.

The Grand Vizier responded that the reputation of the Sultan was already lost, if after having remained so long at a city, where they had consumed so much money, if they withdrew without firing a shot. He said that their artillery was twice as numerous as that of the Christians and if their soldiers lacked experience, it was sufficient that their leaders had it, since the soldiers only needed courage and such leaders at their head. Finally, he said that if the Turks fought resolutely, that was all that could be asked of them. As for the rest, if they did not sustain their honor, at least they would have done their duty and not have fled before the enemy, which would be a shame on them for the rest of their lives.

As the Grand Vizier's opinion served as the law, they acted accordingly. However, the Janissaries did not join them, asking that the siege be raised. In order to get them to return to their duty, they were enticed with greater promises. The next day he reviewed the army, which still contained 110,000 combatants, and having resolved to recall the troops that had been left around Raab and other places in Hungary, he sent others in their place, in whom he did not have as much confidence.

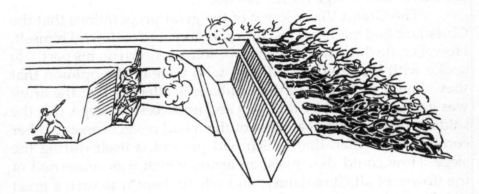

Abatis used to keep the enemy at bay for the longest possible time (Pearson Scott Foreman)

The Christians had decided to attack the Turkish lines, but in order to reach them they had to pass through a wood. From the beginning of the campaign the Christians had taken the precaution of making a large road through this wood in order to be able to pass along it as easily as possible. But the Grand Vizier thought he could inconvenience their passage, so he had it occupied and had sent five or six battalions there, which had constructed a large abatis with trenches. On the other side, the Grand Vizier, after having left 20,000 men to protect his camp and the trenches, came out of his lines with his cavalry and infantry, formed them into three lines, without counting the reserve corps, and had a small rise occupied by some cannon, which could be advantageous during the battle. He then told those on this flank to not abandon their post under any circumstances.

The Christian army, whose commanders had implored divine assistance with public and private prayers, marched with great confidence in their pending victory because they had at their head a prince of such great reputation, who had already defeated the Turks on so many other occasions. However, as much as this circumstance raised the courage of the troops, the fear of the King of Poland weakened that of the Turks as the Turks were more afraid of the Poles than of all the other nations of the world. It would have been easy if the Emperor himself was at the head of his troops, then to have a king, whose fortune and reputation they appreciated. But besides the fact that the Emperor was not so easily committed, the King of Poland had not come so far to obey another, and the Emperor, on his part, could claim to command him, so, the King of Poland remained at Linz, where he had advanced, ordering public prayers in all the churches, asking God with the last fervor that he might favor the arms of the Christians.

When the Christian army arrived at the Vienna Woods the battle began but seeing the Christians did not have much success against the Grand Vizier's men, they sent new men in force to make the fight more difficult. As a result, they threw themselves on the Turkish entrenchments and carried the woods, killing all who were not able to escape. The woods were swept clean and the Christian vanguard placed itself in battle formation in front of the woods to await the arrival of the rearguard, fearing that if it marched forward without having to fight, the Grand Vizier would not advance forward, and the Christians could not profit from his state. The Grand Vizier was careful not to go so far from Vienna, fearing that, while he was on another side, the Christians would move part of their army up the Danube, to attack those he had left to the guard of his lines, which would have too many sorties to resist the garrison at the same time, which never failed to make sortie.

For this reason that he periodically sent detachments to see if the Christians had crossed the Danube. He was further concerned if they had, what he would do on either side, even though he had word that the Christians were marching on him and they would be in action in an hour or two.

It was quite necessary that the relief be close, as the Turks were no longer in the city, but they were digging under it with their mines. Because of this the Count von Starhemberg placed a lamp on the high point of the St. Stephen's Tower, this being the signal agreed to with the Duke of Lorraine that the city was hard pressed. The count's miners were so intimidated that they would barely work, while the garrison, exhausted, was reduced to 5,500 men, of the 16,000 that had started the siege. They had lost 6,000 to the enemy and the rest were lost to sickness, which grew daily. They were no longer taken to their graves one at a time, but a wagon covered with straw was loaded with 10 or 12 and they were dumped into their graves.

Ottoman's attack on Vienna 1683

Those who had escaped from such great peril, and who, in expectation of such a fortune, were almost languishing in death, but knowing that the succor which they had so often hoped for, was on this side of the woods, where it was already seen, took up the arms with so much courage that it was as if they were other men just moments before. They all went on the ramparts, without waiting for any other command than what their courage inspired in them, and it greatly served Starhemberg that they were rejuvenated by this new hope, for those whom the Grand Vizier had left to guard his camp, and those to whom he had given orders to mount the assault, as soon as they saw the enemy coming, they acquitted themselves with so much resolution and firmness, it was very necessary that they should have shown so much of it then, rather than any previous occasion. The Turks, however, who thought that if they repelled this last effort, they were about to be freed from the labors that had so long afflicted them, fought with no less courage; they vigorously defended themselves.

While all this passed, the King of Poland attacked the Grand Vizier, who had advanced before him with more courage than prudence. He had moved away from the post where he had positioned his cannon and from where he could greatly discomfort the Christians. He chose to charge instead of waiting for the attack of the King of Poland. But whatever he thought, be it that he had the advantage in charging first or if he wished to animate the courage of his men, he neglected to take all the normal precautions, which he would soon regret. His troops broke after the first charge and the Christians pursued them hotly, that those that manned the Turkish cannon did not dare to fire out of fear of striking their compatriots.

Starhemberg, warned by the men who he had placed at the high points of the city, that the battle was going favorably for the Christians, launched a sortie by the garrison, which had already chased the Turks from below the rampart. Many of the burghers had mixed with the soldiers to take part in the glory and together they attacked the Turks, who were pillaging their own baggage, having received word that the Grand Vizier's attack had gone badly for him, so they looked to retreat. Everyone, with regret that they had abandoned their tents, thought only of saving themselves, while the Count von Starhemberg at the head of his men, charged them so vigorously that they fell on the retreating Turks. As the lines of circumvallation prevented them from passing as quickly as they desired, they attempted to fill them in, some using their muskets as shovels and others using their hands. They did everything they could to destroy the Turkish siege works. Starhemberg seeing the disorder of the Turks died of regret to profit from this wonderful occasion, but prudence demanded that he not send his troops very far from the city. He contented himself to sending some cavalry after the slowest and remained near the walls, where he continued overseeing the destruction of the Turkish siege works out of fear that the battle might turn against the Christians.

Polish soldiers 1670-1690

These fugitives further augmented the terror of the Grand Vizier's army. The King of Poland had defeated the Turkish wing facing him and the fleeing Turks, abandoned their infantry to the mercy of the Poles, who unhesitatingly rode them down. On the right wing, a bit more resistance was encountered by the Christians, but the Grand Vizier considering that the battle was lost, unable to re-establish it now that the trenches were abandoned, decided to save what remained to him and immediately abandoned his camp, where his tents were still standing, rather than try to save it by a useless obstinacy. With this in mind he ordered the retreat sounded, but the infantry being unable to follow the cavalry, which fled as soon as it heard the retreat sounded, was cut to pieces, and only a quarter of them escaped.

The King of Poland, with a detachment, entered the city to give thanks to God for his victory. Orders were given that there be no pillaging of the abandoned Turkish camp. The Dukes of Bavaria, Saxony, and Lorraine, who had fought with much courage, did the same on their side and assigned a force of 3,000 men to guard the Turkish camp while a council of war was held as to whether they should pursue the fleeing Turks or if they should content themselves with the victory they had achieved. The council was divided. The King of Poland and the Duke of Lorraine, with all that were in the Emperor's party, wished that a pursuit be launched, but the Dukes of Saxony and Bavaria, who had only come to break the siege of Vienna did not wish to risk their troops any further. The Duke of Saxony, who complained that because of his religion, had already been told, that he had to be on his guard, to put his troops into winter quarters in Hungary, where they could engage in intrigues with Thököly, for who the conformity religion were more suspect than all that the Duke of Saxony had just done for the Emperor. This prince, therefore, seeing that, after having traversed a great country, who had hazarded his reputation and even his life, abandoned his dominions, to succor those of others, he was so ill-rewarded, as he received more glory than booty. The Allies, seeing that he was abandoning the common cause in spite of their wishes, gave him a greater share of the booty, which further reduced his displeasure.

The Duke of Bavaria was a little more fortunate, perhaps because the Emperor was apprehensive that in the problems he had with the King of France that the Duke might take sides against him, and, besides that, by the alliance which he had with the Duke, in any case, all the princes not agreeing, a golden bridge was opened for the Turks. The Grand Vizier withdrew to a point near Neuhausel, where he waited for three days for the debris of his army to gather. The Grand Vizier, however, was not unconcerned, how the Grand Lord received news of his defeat, and to save himself, he wrote the Great Lord blaming those who had the principal command after him. It has not yet been learned, however, what the Grand Lord has resolved to do on this subject, nor what the King of Poland has done, whose news is so different, and which he does not know how to judge. However, it is believed, that as great a captain as he is, he knows how to profit by his victory, which all Christians must desire.

Account of the Siege of Vienna Undertaken by the Turks on 15 July

I have employed the first the first person to give you this account of the siege of Vienna that I have prepared for you. My little merit and courage does not permit me to say that I had some part in the wonderful things that occurred here; that it will not be vanity enough to say my prose does justice to what was seen, and that I had done justice to the heroes while presenting the reader with a faithful account of what has happened.

You are no doubt sufficiently informed of the position, the strength, and the importance of this fortress, that I am not obliged to tell you more than it is the capital of Austria and the traditional home of the emperors, situated on a branch of the Danube. It is quite large, of a circular nature, populated with 150,000 souls, decorated with beautiful homes and several magnificent palaces, regularly fortified, and defended by two castles. It contains an extremely well provisioned arsenal and, finally, it has been the objective of the Great Lords (Sultans) since Sulieman II, in 1529, after a siege lasting from 26 September to 14 October, placed the crescent on a tower and left marks of an infamy there which the successors had not been able to wash away until the present.

Thus, the knowledge that you have of all these things gives me the ability to move immediately to what has happened since my arrival, which occurred six months after our separation and 12 April.

I found here everything appropriate for a vigorous defense, on the receipt of the news of the extraordinary preparations of the Porte. The magazines were filled with all munitions; materials were brought in for works completed outside the walls; some that were lacking were begun; razing the suburbs was discussed and it was decided to leave them standing for the moment, but that they would have to be destroyed if the enemy approached.

Affairs remained in this state until the Prince of Lorraine arrived at the head of the Imperial army (June 1683) and he was sent part of the cannons from Vienna, plus ammunition, and the construction of the newly started works was ceased (the material filling, in some locations, the ditches) in the hope that if the troops of the Emperor did nothing better, at least they would stop the war in Hungary.

After various accidents, which occurred to our army, you have learned, no doubt, that the towns and villages for three or four leagues around were on fire, and continuous bodies of fugitives, fleeing before the Turks, told us stories of the cruelties exercised on all who fell in their hands. We had never seen such consternation. Everyone thought themselves lost; there were only complaints against the government. All was lamentations and despair. I have no doubt that if the Grand Vizier was as close to Vienna as the Tartars, the bourgeois would have sent him a deputation to seek a favorable settlement.

In order to raise morale of the people, the government employed wasted remedies. They used threats against those who spoke badly about the state of things, they provided public prayers in the churches twice a day to beseech God's forgiveness; frequent sermons were given to justify the actions of the ministers and to dissipate the terror. Many of those in the suburbs could no longer live there and they withdrew into the city, including the Empress-Dowager. Others did not even dare to remain in the city, abandoned everything and fled. Those who remained resolved to put up a resistance and began taking steps to defend themselves. This included consenting to the destruction of the suburbs from which there was much to fear, while others worked to clean out the moat of materials and to prefect some half completed works as much as time permitted.

The Emperor now looked to repair his mistake of sending part of the city's cannon and ammunition off with the Duke of Lorraine. As for the cannon, he could do nothing as we had enough and for provisions, there came a considerable quantity by the Danube as well as powder, shot, and other things that dazzled the citizenry.

Until this point the Turks were still some distance away, but on 7 July, from the army of Prince Charles of Lorraine, the Count of Stirum[10] sent General Carrara, and the Count de Montecuculi to bring news to the Emperor of the rout of his troops on Schut Island and informed him that beyond the prisoners, more than 3,000 infantry had been killed and almost all the army's baggage had been lost. The rest of the army stood on the island as if besieged, but that the cavalry had separated from the army in

---

[10]Herman Otto II of Limburg Stirum (1646 – 1704)

disorder and had reached Kitzee. After the Grand Vizier, crossed the bridge at Essek on 30 June he had a long conference with Count Thököly. On the third of the month he had camped at Stuffenburg while several cities in Hungary had joined the opposition party[11]; that they had abandoned several others to save the garrisons, which could not have defended them; that the Turks had gathered all their troops and had begun to march on Vienna.

This news was debated in the palace in order to conceal it from the people. But various fugitives, who reached Vienna as they avoided capture by the barbarians, spread the news in the streets that was not spoken of in the Supreme Council: that the Turks were masters of Raab, Gomorre, and Pressburg, as well as all of Hungary; that they were only two days from Vienna and numbered more than 200,000. As one can imagine, all was despair and terror. Terrible passions produced ridiculous effects that no authority could stop.

The Emperor deliberated on what action to take. His council represented to him that he should consider leaving the city. This departure could only be kept from the people for only a few days; while remaining would only expose him to the insults of a terrified population. If the Turks, knew he was in the city, they would redouble their efforts to destroy the Empire in a single blow. Further, if he was besieged in the city he could not communicate with the world powers, which he needed, to hasten the relief from the Circles [of Germany][12] and Poland; that he could not gather the necessary materials nor remedy the thousand ills that frequently occur among the corps that are not held by a single superior authority. On the contrary, if he withdrew to Linz, he could direct and address all these needs. Finally, that the Emperor would find his tomb within the walls of a besieged city.

---

[11]The Kuruc were anti-Habsburg Hungarians in Royal Hungary that opposed the Empire from 1671 – 1711.

[12]Translator: During the Early Modern period the Holy Roman Empire was divided into Imperial Circles, administrative groupings whose primary purposes were the organization of common defensive structures and the collection of imperial taxes but were also used as a means of organization within the Imperial Diet and the Imperial Chamber Court. Each circle had a Circle Diet, although not every member of the Circle Diet would hold membership of the Imperial Diet as well. The circles were the Bavarian Circle, Franconian Circle, Saxon Circle, Swabian Circle, Upper Rhenish Circle, Westphalian Circle, the Austrian Circle, the Burgundian Circle and the Electoral Rhenish Circle.

Though the Emperor was truly touched by this advice, he none-theless found it a shameful thing to flee, but his wife the Empress, was in tears and in a pitiful state, as she was in an advanced state of pregnancy. She refused to leave the Emperor's side and even-tually this convinced him to leave.

The Emperor left by the Nieuburg Cloister at 9:00 p.m. with the two empresses, the archdukes and the archduchesses, but in such a great disorder that he only took some jewels and some papers with him; and he was only escorted by some of the officers of his household and foreign ministers. The latter fled in great disorder with the Emperor and were not in a state to defend him. The danger that he ran was not small. The Tartars had pre-ceded him almost everywhere spreading fire and steel, lighting his way with terrible flames. If he had encountered a group of as few as 200 of them, he would have been lost.

The departure of the Emperor caused the same of all the richest merchants, the great burghers, and an infinity of other people. No one opposed them, because there was no force to do so and it was beneficial to get rid of so many superfluous mouths. Those who fled took only their money and abandoned their pro-visions and other things that were useless.

The next day, at daybreak, another shock arrived when we saw Prince Charles of Lorraine before the city's gates at the head of his cavalry along with the Count von Starhemberg, our governor. In addition, there was Count von Capliers, recalled from Krembs by the Emperor to preside over the Council of War, the Duke von Croy, and several other officers destined to fight the siege of Vienna. Perhaps because their presence prevented the seditious from spreading rumors or be it because they raised the crushed spirits of the populace, as when in the most pressing dangers one ordinary abandons oneself to the least beam of hope, whatever it may be, the city quickly changed from extreme anxi-ety to a state of calm. They listened to all that was said about the retreat of the Emperor. They followed all orders that were issued and everyone, officers, soldiers, bourgeois, churchmen, women and children set to working with such fervor on the palisades that they were finished on the 12th.

Unexpectedly, on the 11th, Count Esterhazy Palatin of Hungary arrived. He had been abandoned by all his troops who had passed over to Thököly and had only brought his household with him in a very sad state. This arrival caused great disorder. A few troublemakers cried loudly that Turks would give quarter to those who surrendered; that to resist them was to lead to great misfortune. Many listened and rumors began to spread. However, the calm and wisdom of the leaders appeased the crowd. They attempted to convince the people that a siege was not certain and to them to prepare for war, and then they began to execute what had been ordered in the council, to which the best intended magistrates and burgomasters were sometimes invited. During the night of the 13th/14th the city was on the point of surrendering to the Turks before they had arrived. The Scottish Monastery caught fire and the fire consumed the houses on both sides of the Lord's Street, reaching Herrenstrasse near the arsenal. It was only stopped with great effort. The true cause of the fire was never discovered, but some Hungarians were accused. This served to enhance the rage of the people against Thököly who it was thought had sought to open the city to the Grand Vizier by the fire. I also believe it augmented their desire to defend it.

On the 15th, our scouts reported that the Turks had left their camp at Kitzee and were advancing on us, being only a day's march away. On receiving this news, Prince Charles assembled the city council and said that the city would soon be besieged, but if anyone wished to protect the city and provide correspondence, he would leave them some men to defend them but the rest would move a bit away to protect the Vienna Bridge and by the same means maintain communications with his other troops who were beyond the Danube. He would return on the first with the relief forces from the Circles and Poland and then his troops would be stronger than those of the infidels, they would beat them in their presence, or at least force them to raise the siege.

The thought of a siege by the Turks occupied the minds of the inhabitants again, but more sharply than ever. They listened only to the words of the prince. Terror spread throughout the city and people ran about without knowing where to go. However, the Prince of Lorraine entered the fortress with some dragoons and a part of his infantry, which had arrived in the suburbs a few days earlier. He moved his army, about 24,000 men, from the side of Pressburg avoiding an encounter with the Turks. That same evening, from the tower of St. Stephan (the bell tower of the cathedral raised in the form of a pyramid to the height of 480 degrez) lookouts spotted the vanguard of the Grand Vizier's army. Shortly after this the rest of it appeared and one heard the sounds of the barbarians. The Vienna I saw before me at this time suggested to me it would have been lost if it were not for the wisdom and the conduct of the Governor, the Count von Star-hemberg . Further, I dare to advance the idea that His Imperial Majesty owes the salvation of Austria to the choice that he had made by selecting this great man.

Paul, Prince Esterházy (1635 -1713)

When this brave count entered, after having accompanied Prince Charles of Lorraine to the edge of the suburb, the first thing that he did, among the absolute confusion that reigned everywhere, was to visit the ramparts, to put good men in position, and then to ride through the streets to calm the public and cause them to return to their homes. However, the pitiful cries of the women and children threw despair into the hearts of the firmest hearted. Part of the night was spent in a council of war where the Governor learned the state of affairs and what yet had to be done. In the early morning, he ordered that all the corps of troops of the city should assemble at the grand place of the New Market. He appeared there richly armed and superbly mounted, presenting himself in a heroic air to fire the courage of those he could and to silence the others. He said only these few words:

"Gentlemen, it is not necessary to talk, but to act. You see also to what we are reduced and to what we are resolved. For me, since I have been given the honor of defending this fortress, I promise that the enemy will never become its master, until they have trod on my dead body in the breach. And if so many brave people as are here, wish only to follow me, where I would go, I have this confidence in God that this misfortune will not arrive. But, gentlemen, as it is perhaps necessary to suffer and expose ourselves, and those who do not wish to do this are only useless mouths, of which we have no need, and the plagues of the cities besieged by false alarms that spread everywhere: I declare that if there are any in Vienna, who are not ready to spill their last drop of blood, before they surrender, he is permitted to leave this morning. I shall open a gate and I will give him an escort to Linz. However, if after this time anyone who remains dares to speak of capitulation, I will build sufficient gallows to punish them."

One sees how much the eloquence of a man of authority and the people are changed. That of Vienna, however, quickly returned to its alarm, responding to this short harangue with cries of "They want to die, not to surrender." Count von Starhemberg, gave time for the people to decide what they wished to do, went to organize other things and returned two hours later, followed by a crowd of people crying "We wish to die with you." Charmed by this unanimous resolution of everyone, which was more apparent on their faces than in their protestations, the Count said that he: "...was pleased to tell them beforehand of their peril, in order not to retain in the city those who did not fear anyone; that, since they were all as they wished, it was now just to give them knowledge that they had but little to fear. The infidels were already fatigued, and their too great multitude would soon starve them, as they could not receive food either from their country which was too far away, and nothing had escaped the ravages of the Tartars; that this destruction, after having caused so many evils in Austria, would in part be the cause of its salvation. While the siege lasted, they would be defending a fortress from which their fathers had driven out the same enemies, who had greater numbers, and under a much more redoubtable general, who was the Vizier when it was not fortified in the way that it was now. His Imperial Majesty, who justified his retreat showing that it was necessary and advantageous, would bring forward the relief from the Circles and Poland once all the troops were united, they would attack the besiegers, and they would invariably defeat them. They would have the pleasure of saving their goods, their children, their religion, their liberty, their lives, and see themselves called by all of Europe, whose eyes were on them, with the same glory as their ancestors, the illustrious defenders of the Faith and Germany. They should consider all these reasons and in them they would find the memory of their courage. If they wished to throw their eyes to the other side, they would not be unaware of the treatment ordinarily given to those they have been defeated. They had less to fear or instead more to desire, which was to die honorably with their arms in hand for the defense of religion and homeland. That they died gloriously before men and full of merit before God! Death not daring to ask for himself, because his life was necessary to them, he wished to his best friends.

Then he spoke with the same force, having received a thousand applauds from the garrison, who had tears in their eyes and placed faith in their salvation in such a great man with their cries of approval. He asked for everyone, to assure each other, that they were willing to swear formally to die or to save the fortress. A hundred thousand arms were raised to the sky and the oath was taken as they took the most sacred oath.

After this, the Governor held a most private assembly, that included only the principal magistrate and the bourgeoisie with the captains of the quarters. He gave them their orders, which he had already worked out with the Count de Capliers, who had recommended their execution.

They gathered money, which was deposited in the communities, promised to be repaid after the siege, and made a fund to support the garrison. The state of all provisions was made; including those in public magazines, as well as those held by private individuals, and made them all common, sealing granaries and cellars. A price was set for all things; drums were beaten to place all bourgeois, students, shop boys, lackeys, etc under arms. The shop boys were promised the rights of the bourgeoisie, and the others a reward proportional to their condition. The craftsmen, the workmen, the prisoners, etc., were made ready for the necessities, and put under captains. Three hospitals were established for the wounded in three religious houses. The religious were assigned various employers, besides those who make it their profession; such as treating the sick, making bullets and fascines, and repair work. It was forbidden under the grievous punishment to perform useless plays, while in the churches, there were daily sermons and public prayers. Gibbets are raised in various quarters of the city, to catch those who spoke of surrender without remission. Various affairs are regulated by public posters.

After these things were taken into account of all the troops, the garrison found itself composed of 30,000 men, among which were 8,000 of the ordinary garrision, 12,000 detached from the Imperial Army, 7,000 burghers, 1,000 students, 1,000 shop boys, and 4,000 lackeys or valets. The Count von Starhemberg drew weapons from the arsenal for those who had none. He also ordered that everyone be given a ration of bread and wine per day. He established their pay and distributed an advance.

Then he positioned troops in all the places they were needed. Next, he made sure that all the posts had a mix of experienced men and those who had not experienced war in order that the latter might learn from the others and he ignited among them a noble emulation that produces the most wonderful actions.

From the garrison, he turned his concerns to working on machines and artifices of war. An engineer named Kimpler, a most skillful man, had the stewardship of everything. The other engineers were under him, as were several artisans and workers who had placed themselves under the flags, as we have said. They were employed in the arsenal. The rest, in waiting for the besiegers to furnish other concerns worked on some works to serve as entrenchments in locations that appeared weak. On the other hand the clergy, the churchmen, the magistrates, and the people were led by their leaders in long and very devout processions to the Church of the Augustines; where everybody together, at the feet of Our Lady of Lorette, to whom they prayed as their protector from the Turks, they solemnly vowed certain priests to pray every day for the intercession of the Virgin Mary for the deliverance of the city. The most celebrated devotion of Austria was that of Our Lady of Lorette. The people of Vienna surpassed all others by their confidence in her.

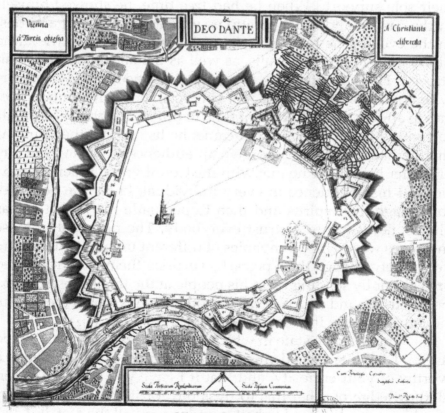

Vienna in 1683.

So many different members of so great a body were thus applied to a employment according to his ability, and thus placed in that position; it was the objective of the Governor to maintain them there. This incomparable man addressed everything. He was always armed and in good spirits. He anticipated everything, ordered everything, and assisted in everything. Maybe it will not be disagreeable to you if I tell you he was busy every day.

He ordinarily slept in his armor at midnight. After two or three hours at most of a light sleep, he mounted his horse and moved to the guard and visited, in person, the sentries. From there he went where entrenchments were being constructed, then to the arsenal to examine the diligence and the work of the workers in one or other location. He rarely failed to make a tour of the city to show himself to the people, who regarded him as their sole support. When he had free time, he showed himself in the castles and other locations, where there were garrisons. In the evening he repeated part of his travels, but above all he did not fail to tour the walls, as well as the alleys and the main streets. He was affable to everyone and encouraged everyone with good words or some act of generosity. When wounded began to appear, he moved from time to time through the hospitals to console them. When night came, he listened to the opinions that he had been unable to give an audience to during the day and after his dinner he met with the Count von Capliers. He expressed his confidence in every individual, knew the best way to manage their spirits and then to persuade them, that it was always necessary to distrust everybody. The principal of these measures was to mix companies of different units as sentinels; to very rarely change their posts; to surprise them by unexpected arrivals, or by sending them his people at the times they least expected them; and of doing various other things which the skillful captain's practice in these encounters.

This was the state in which Vienna constantly maintained itself. I have stretched myself there because I have judged it worthy of your curiosity, and that if I gave you at first a general knowledge of what this fortress did for its defense, not only would you be disposed to better understand all the rest, but also that I may afterwards attach myself only to the account of the principal particularities, and to avoid those annoying repetitions which render the relations of sieges so course and ill-ordered. It is now time to look at the enemy whom we left behind when he arrived before Vienna on the 15 July.

It was during the evening and there was nothing to note beyond the normal practices of the Turks. They uttered thunderous voices, and those who advanced to the walls, fired arrows, to some of which they had attached notes full of threats. But the next day it would have been an infinitely agitated spectacle to see them arrange their tents, if we could take care of the thought, that these preparations were made against our lives. The news of the truest kind made the number rise to 180,000 men, composed of 110,000 Janissaries or Spahis, 40,000 Tartars, and other nations submitting to the Porte.

Their camp was organized like a pretty city where everything was ordered with symmetry. The streets were long, wide, and straight. There were spacious squares. Pavilions replaced houses and they were so rich and so brilliant that no such thing was ever seen in the Christian armies. The various quarters were occupied by corps or of different nations, or of different employment, such as the headquarters, where the Grand Vizier and his favorites resided, and the pleasure palace of the Empress Dowager. The Turkish camp extended from the edge of the Danube by Vienna to Nusdorf. They dug no entrenchments believing that no one would dare to approach them and that they would take the city quickly.

They remained a few days, be it to reconnoiter the fortress, to prepare for the attack or to point their cannon. At 5:00 p.m., the terrible thunder erupted with a general discharge of all their batteries together - they had prepared several. The three principal ones were in the Prader facing three different ports. They were served with marvelous care by 700 gunners, almost all renegades from various nations. They fired without pause, but their guns were mediocre and appeared to be more to intimidate the besieged than to beat down their walls. Several shots went wide while others did not produce any great effect. The people of Vienna soon became accustomed to the noise and lost their fear of it. What the Turks had intended to shake them only served to strengthen them.

An Austrian soldier in the 1680's

The Count von Starhemberg began with two actions. He caused counter-batteries to be set up which counter the Turks' cannon, though not quite early on. Secondly, in order to prepare the courage of the garrison for this enterprise of importance, which he was contemplating, he ordered a sortie to take a party of Tartars, who had gone to forage. At another time it might have been funny to see the inhabitants mixed with some companies of the Mansfeld and Hensler Regiments. They went, and their wives accompanied them, as to death, resolved, nevertheless, to perish, but to sell their lives dearly. Those who led them, executed the orders that they should not engage them too closely. The Governor knew well that the Tartars would not stand; and he did not claim a great victory, but his men took heart for more hazardous actions. Indeed, when those who had stayed behind saw their companions come back safe and sound, they were ashamed not to have gone, and they ardently demanded to go out. Those who had gone were proud of their attempt and in order to support their reputation, which they had acquired, they were now were the first to run to danger, so that those who hitherto believed that it was a great deal for them to stand guard, in the future thought it nothing at all, if they did not duly fulfill all the other duties as soldiers. They soon needed their resolution, which they seized.

The Grand Vizier, in order to profit from the first ardor of his men, before it relented, as he did not doubt, on the advice given to him by others, acted to take the fortress without waiting for a practicable breach and launched three assaults before 24 July.

A handgrenade from the 17th century

During the night that preceded the first assault there was so much activity in the Turkish camp that it was easy for us to determine the cause. We were, as a result, prepared to give a strong resistance when, at daybreak, the Turkish cannon ceased firing. We then heard the sound of an infinity of warrior's instruments, many of which we did not use. We then saw several battalions of Janissaries detach from the army that were supported on their flanks by some squadrons of Spahis (which served as little more than a parade). This force advanced towards our walls between the Schotenburg Gate and the Red Tower. Their demeanor was very proud, their cries terrible, and their numbers sufficiently large to cause our men to tremble. But, our bourgeois, only this time, did not do all that they had promised. The attack began with a cloud of arrows, which whistled through the air and this was all. This was accompanied by a discharge of musketry, which barely did any damage at all. They had to come closer and then began a marvelous action, which the confusion concealed from us. Our cannon constantly fired on those who came from the Turkish camp to assist their companions. Our musketeers and grenadiers[13] performed marvels. The engineer Kimpler fired artifices, which were a new invention.[14] Our veteran regiments fought for some time with pike and sword. However, our governor wished to show on this occasion that which one would hope from him on other occasions. He was at the head of those who needed encouragement or a push. He gave all the orders and one can say that he stirred all arms, that he struck all the blows, which was quite different from several captains, who had the glory of great actions, and who had not frequently contributed to the actions of those who served under their authority. In this first assault and throughout the siege, his soldiers and officers merited no other honor by the exploits that they had executed, but of having given their themselves to serve as the instrument of the genius who gave them movement and vigor. The combat was relentless for more than six hours with much fury on both parts. The Turks were finally obliged to leave after suffering heavy losses, which was augmented further by a sortie by the cavalry, which struck them during their retreat.

The second assault occurred at the same hour, the same location, in the same manner, and had the same success as the first. The difference was only that the fury and the multitude of the Turks was greater; that our resistance was even greater, and the armed inhabitants were overly attentive spectators who did not know what to do. A single company of shoemaker apprentices led by an old captain drove back all of a battalion of Turks. There is nothing impossible in necessity and in a determined resolution to sell one's life dearly.

Some of this militia gained experienced at their own expense, but new courage needs to be moderated by experience. They had joined a detachment of a part of the Schaffemberg and Starhemberg Regiments, sent to cut off part of the Turks, who

---

[13]Grenadiers carried grenades which were small round balls filled with gunpowder and ignited by a fuse which was lit, then thrown.

[14]Translator. These "artifices" are probably mines that were dug under probable lines of approach, filled with gunpowder, and detonated when the enemy was over top of them.

came from the side of Thabor to rejoin their army. After having defeated the most advanced part of this force, they wished to pursue the others, against the orders of their commanders, and became disorganized in the process. On their return they found themselves cut off by some troops that had been sent from the camp, and they could not rally. Many of them saved themselves as best they could, while others preferred to throw themselves into the Danube rather than fall into the Turks' hands. This disaster did not cool the ardor of their companions, but it served to make them more susceptible to discipline. This appeared in the third attack.

The Ottoman army began its third attack without cries and instruments of war, but with many more attackers than the two other assaults. Auxiliaries marched first, in order that they might fatigue the garrision and the completely fresh Janissaries could renew the combat, which hopefully the garrison could not sustain. This tactic had frequently served the Turks well in the past, this time only produced more deaths among their men. All of Vienna stirred that day. The Governor resembled a bolt of lightning, so quickly did he appear and disappear everywhere, and he did much execution. Mansfeld's battalions, were commanded by the Count de Lesle, and part of the Württemberg Regiment received and valiantly withstood all the efforts of the Turks. The platoons of the militia that had been posted in the towers, from where they had come upon the attack, fired on the Turks. The others, who had been taught to throw grenades used their training to good effect. The artisans and workers threw firebombs, which they had prepared. The women and children came for the first time, bringing refreshments to their husbands and fathers.

The priests and churchmen, some carrying who they were told to carry, the others taking the wounded and transporting them to the hospitals. Finally, the salvation of the city depended on its resistance and it was necessary that it be extraordinary, because the Turks, who were driven back several times, kept coming. Wave after wave succeeded each other marching on the stomachs of the dead and dying like as if on a level road. The officers were the first, giving an arm to help their soldiers or standing behind them with sabers in hand, to prevent them from withdrawing. It was only after seven or eight hours of combat that they had to fall back. The garrison pursued them and killed many in the disorder of their retreat. In these three assaults, the Turks lost about 8,000 to 9,000 men. The defenders of the city lost 500 dead or wounded.

While the city celebrated with its ordinary marks of pleasure, a *chiaoux*[15] arrived who asked to speak with the Governor. The Count, who saw all the inhabitants swollen with their success and full of hope for the future wished to hear this envoy in public. His commission was to propose, on the part of the Grand Vizier, a suspension of arms to recover the dead and to make promises advantageous to all if they wished to capitulate. Otherwise, there would be no quarter for anyone. The valiant Starhemberg scornfully rejected the *chiaoux*'s propositions. Not only did he refuse the truce but returned the prisoners to the *chiaoux* with orders to say to the vizier that he would return all the other prisoners if he wished to send them forward in an assault. The rumor ran that the commission cost this poor Turk dearly and when he wished to acquit himself, the Grand Vizier responded with the blow of his saber which removed his head.

A grenadier in the 17th century

The Governor having thus addressed the Turkish envoy, he turned to the people and said to them: "That the infidels had asked for a truce because they fear that the dead bodies will spread corruption into their camps, and he did not wish to accord it to them until this had happened. One could see by the submissions of such a proud enemy, the confidence that they should conceive,

[15]A sub-commander of the Janissaries

that they should act with the same ardor and the same union as they had to that point."

Cries of joy interrupted him and were only stopped by the arrival of the principal burgomasters. After having rendered solemn prayers thanking God and the Virgin Mary in the Augustines, they came publicly to honor their illustrious defender. He expressed to them much gratitude for their civility; he praised them for their zeal and then spoke modestly of himself. Finally, he recommended to them that they continue as they had done and above all, to contain the inconstancy of the timid and changeable populace; this was only fault from which there was reason to fear for Vienna.

From 24 July into August the Turks battered the fortress with more fury, never interrupting it, except during the intervals of the assaults. They had also constructed a new battery at the Spanish Cloister before the Scottish Gate. The Austrian cannon, well served, however, and ruined this battery along with many others. On our side the Governor wished to profit from the ardor full of boldness that inspired the men from their first success at war and executing an important enterprise which we mentioned earlier that he was contemplating.

The Jewish suburb called Leopoldstadt had not been burned and from the beginning of the siege, as the Austrians were occupied with defending the city's wall, the Turks had captured it. Count von Starhemberg thought this post was useful to them and resolved to take it. He chose the Starhemberg Regiment for this task and attached a company of dragoons to it, with a force of militia, which had pressed him to participate. After finding this action worthy of his courage and his conduct, he prepared to lead it himself. The prayers of all the officers and tears of the Viennese who were present, expressed their fears of losing him and could barely prevent him from going. He gave command to Count von Souches, a captain who merited commanding when Count von Starhemberg was not present. This force surprised the Turks, who had not expected an attack and had not entrenched themselves. The Austrians pushed the Turks foot-by-foot to the edge of the suburb on the side of their army. There the Austrians found more resistance. They would have overcome it, however, had not some detachments from the Turkish camp arrived. It then was necessary for the Austrians to think of holding the ground they had gained, and they now set about defending their conquest. Five hundred young students, who were there, showed that the Muses do not restore their infants, as they say. The Turks, who, in order to be better warriors, renounced all the sciences, learned at their expense, that ignorance may well make a man more ferocious, but that he does not do it courageously. Count von Souches fulfilled, on his part, all the duties of a skillful captain. He harassed the enemy, made entrenchments, and lodged a small garrison in a small fort. But what terminated this undertaking gloriously, was the bold action of a dragoon. This brave man noticed a Turk more advanced than the others, and who, with more appearance, showed much more heart than his fellows. Driven by a generous impetuousness, he darted out of the ranks, and with his saber in his hand, and with a reverse stroke cut off the Turk's head, and then he returned to his post. The Turks lost heart and withdrew from the suburb, returning to their camp with cries of lamentation. We soon learned that the man the dragoon had killed was a well-regarded Pasha and close friend of the Grand Vizier because of his rare military talents. Though the Turks held a part of Leopoldstadt, the Viennese remained masters of the rest.

All these events showed the Grand Vizier that Vienna was not a fortress to be taken as easily as he had promised. We learned from prisoners that the Count Serin had persuaded him that this city was unable to resist longer; that it was a result of his council that the Grand Vizier had resumed the siege; that, in order to capture it he had employed his best soldiers, of whom he suffered a very great loss; that the prize of the same Count von Serin and the discovery of his treason had disconcerted him utterly; that if he had thought that the garrison would have defended itself so vigorously, he might not have attacked it. But he had committed the honor of the Ottoman name with so much noise that it was absolutely necessary to succeed in his enterprise. With this intention he wanted to initially test the firmness of the Governor, and for that reason he sent him, for a second time, an envoy bearing very reasonable offers, and in case of refusal of the threats to flay him alive and to spare neither sex nor age. Starhemberg's answer was worthy of his great heart: He said that he was very certain that he would only be flayed if he was dead, but before that he had advised the Grand Vizier to watch out for his own skin and to not presume that it would be so easy for him to reduce to his will people who did not fear him.

The Turkish general then turned his thoughts to more effective means. To this point he had in his actions more fury than conduct; that by not attacking in the normal manner, he had gained nothing; and not having made any entrenchments in his camp, he perceived that he could be surprised by the Duke of Lorraine, whose army was growing daily. Wishing therefore to act in an orderly manner, he began to have his men dig large and deep ditches around his camp, except on the side of the Danube. He entrenched himself and after that he dug covered walkways and employed several peasants as slaves to do the work.

These things occupied all his attention and his artillery did not fire until 24 July. The Count von Starhemberg did not let this time pass in idleness. He had the trenches repaired and dug new ones and had cadavers thrown towards the enemy. He had tall houses that overlooked the Prader cut down and placed cannon in them. But what was most important was that he placed mines underground which were most beneficial. After all this had been done it was important to send news to the Imperial Army and inform it of the good state of the fortress. However, the Turks had blocked all the avenues so well that it had been impossible at this point to send out anyone. A fisherman risked slipping out by swimming the Danube on the 26th and he had the good fortune to cross and return without impediment.

The letters which Prince Charles of Lorraine gave him, indicated that his troops were three leagues away, between Vienna and Pressburg. They were in good condition, increasing in number every day, and awaiting the assistance which would come to them from all quarters. Baron Degenfeld was already advancing with 9,000 Bavarians, the Duke of Saxony brought more Saxons and the other Circles had also raised their levies. The King of Poland would soon set out to help and if Vienna still held out, it would not be long before the siege was raised. General Dunewald and Count Taff, who were cutting off almost all the convoys sent to the Turks' camp, had just cut a party of 6,000 Tartars to pieces, taking all their booty. That the Count von Serin (Chamberlain of the Emperor and Countess Thököly's brother), in an abominable act of treason, had put himself at the head of 8,000 Tartars, to seize the treasure of His Imperial Majesty, which was ascending the Danube. After the defeat of his troops near the Vienna Woods, he was taken prisoner to Linz. At this point the Turks, already almost without food, would soon start deserting; and every day saw the ranks of the Tartars diminish, as they were good only to plunder, and unable to remain in the lines before a city. They started to disengage themselves from the Ottoman army.

This news was read publicly and pleased everyone. The Governor, however, held it a secret that Count von Serin had promised the Grand Vizier that he would give Vienna over to him. This information disturbed the count. In this extremity he did not make it known to anyone, as he had always done. There never appeared anything that marked this collusion, or that the vigilance of the Governor was too ill-intended. It seems the capture of Count von Serin caused them to change their plan; or that, as is probable, there was really no one who came to an understanding with him.

In the meantime, the Turks had begun to make new, vigorous efforts that were better organized than the previous. But as my letter is already longer than I had intended, and as I had not undertaken to write you other than information about the siege that you can read without boredom, I shall admit the boring details with which one ordinarily loads accounts of this kind of subject.

The Turks established their principal attack on the side of the Danube against counterscarp which they had repeatedly attempted to occupy. Nothing can be imagined, that they did not wish to overcome, or that the besieged did not miss in order to save themselves. Fortune seemed rather doubtful. In order to oblige, fortune come to a decision, they often came to blows with a sword. On this occasion I cannot overlook the heroic action of the wife of a good Viennese craftsman. She loved him only, and she could not suffer him to expose himself. One day on the counterscarp he was the most advanced. She came and arrived just as a Janissary gave him a mortal blow. He was focused on his attack and did not see the danger in which he was placed. She tore the sword from the dying husband's hands, and plunged it into his murderer, giving his soul a free passage to follow and embrace the shadows of Hades.

At the same time as the Turks did not succeed in advancing on this side, they had more success on the other. They regarded it as a very great dishonor that the Viennese had taken Leopoldstadt. As a result, they sent many men to retake it and after a stubborn resistance, when the defenders saw that sooner or later they would have to surrender the suburb, as they had too much ground to cover inside their walls, without elongating and exposing people to unnecessary risk, they set the suburb on fire and withdrew in good order.

Images of Kuruc Hungarian rebels (wikipedia)

People, who are never led by reason, however, were soon angry at the loss of Leopoldstadt but soon consoled themselves. A few Turks detached from the camp were feeding the cattle too quietly and too near us for their safety. Men saw this from the ramparts, conceiving the plan of attacking them, and carrying off the herd. It was executed and a hundred head of cattle were brought into the city where meat could only be bought at a very high price, but the city's joy was overwhelming.

The city had a greater reason to rejoice, however; that being the bad state of the Ottoman army. The latter had lost many of its best officers and soldiers at the counterscarp and yet his attack was still more than 40 paces away. Food and forage were already lacking. The Tartars continued to desert. The Ottoman army was heavily dependent on fruit for food, which produced a dysentery which had killed nearly 1,700 men. Corpses were exposed over a number of miles, and the earth stirred up by the covered roads in the places where the dead of the last plague had been buried, which also caused such a great infection that several battalions had been moved a league and a half away. We even believed that the whole camp would also be moved away, so great was the stench that it could kill a man.

These incidents convinced the Grand Vizier that he had been deceived by the report that had told him it would be easy to take Vienna. Nevertheless, this served only to make him more determined to take the city whatever the price. That is why he pressed the mining effort. He established six new batteries and summoned the fortress to surrender for a third time, but with a threat. He said that if he was forced to take it by assault, he would put them all to death, including women and children. When the city refused, he promised the pillage of the city to his troops in order to animate them.

When informed of all these things, Count von Starhemberg sent word to Prince Charles and added that his spies and the prisoners had informed him that the Turks were awaiting the arrival of 20,000 Janissaries and other troops from Asia. If all these joined the siege force, he would need immediate relief; but if the Turks did nothing better than they had to this point, he could hold out for another two months. His envoy, who disguised himself as a Turk, was as successful as the fisherman. On his return he carried very good news; that being that the Imperial troops beyond the Danube continued to stop the convoys coming to the Turkish siege forces; that the garrison of Raab had seized a large number of horses and camels; and that in awaiting relief His Imperial Majesty was preparing to send us gunpowder, shot, grenades and other things we would soon be lacking. All this material was placed in barges on the Danube and almost all of them arrived safely. The Turks had been able to seize only one or two of the last barges.

However, what brought the city's joy to a peak was the holding of Pressburg. It had falsely been thought that it had surrendered to Thököly a long time ago without it being possible to hide it from the inhabitants of Vienna. At this time, it was truly on the point of falling into the Turks' hands. The townsfolk had received passes from Thököly; his troops had already united with those of the Pashas from Javarin and Agria, who were almost in a position to force the Imperial garrison, which was in the castle; when, at that moment, Prince Charles arrived and attacked the army of the Turks and rebels. He tore them to pieces, capturing a large number of wagons loaded with ammunition and baggage; took an *aga*, one of Tekely's secretaries, and a Hungarian count who soon died of his wounds as prisoners. He then fortified the city's garrison, left the ammunition in the castle and set things so right that the Hungarians, who in universal alarm had abandoned the Empire, returned in great numbers.

After his success, Prince Charles wished to inform Count von Starhemberg and as soon as his envoy entered the city, a signal was given from the St. Stephens Tower by three cannon shots, which we later learned caused much alarm in the Grand Vizier's camp.

The Grand Vizier employed all means possible to sustain the courage of his army and to carry by force the city of Vienna before the Christian relief army was in a position to fight. He announced that the Great Lord was preparing to come in person to the camp with 50,000 newly raised troops. He also said that he had at last received his heavy cannon and heavy mortars. He prepared two new batteries, one near the Spanish Cloister and the other near the Red Tower near the Barrier Bridge where he began a continuous fire. The Governor of Vienna sensing that these two locations had the roofs removed from several houses that overlooked these two batteries and posted cannon there to fire on the breaching batteries. He also gave all the orders necessary to fortify the most exposed places and to receive the enemy with vigor. None of these efforts were useless. Three days after they prepared their batteries, the Turks fired their first mine with success and rushed into the path it had cleared for them with such fury that the defenders killed many of them but could not hold the counterscarp. Since this was the first success that they could claim to have gained, they received it with joy and uttered great cries of victory. They did not know, no doubt, that victory and death are often separated by an inch of ground and that when one has only gained half a victory one is also half in the tomb. Before they could entrench themselves in the ground that they had gained, the engineer Kimpler[16] fired two mines that succeeded as anticipated. Most of the Turks who had lodged themselves in the counterscarp were buried. The others attempted to maintain themselves there, but Starhemberg led forward his forces and drove them out once again. He had posted two small cannon and some musketeers in two demi-lunes on the side of the counterscarp. With their continual fire they killed many Turks when they attacked and when they were repulsed.

This is how the conduct and valor of Count von Starhemberg led at the beginning of August. He subsequently encountered greater difficulties that he needed to overcome. Sometimes the garrison seemed to lose heart; spies had often insinuated themselves into the city. There were defectors who passed every day to the Turks' camp; some people began to dare to complain; and as there might seem to be nothing more to cause him pain, he was suffering from dysentery. But the obstacles do nothing against a hero, who has put into practice his virtue, in order that it may appear more brilliantly. You'll see it.

The Turks chased from the counterscarp resumed the fire of their guns with more ferocity than before. But when they saw that our cannon against the effect of their cannon, they turned to mining between the Karndren and Bouriken Gates, using not only their miners, but peasants brought from the lands subject to the Great Lord and all the captives they had in their camp. On 8 August everything was ready to detonate two mines. A part of the ravelin was destroyed, carrying away a captain and 50 soldiers. The Turks thought that all the ravelin had collapsed into the moat and in this belief, they crossed the counterscarp, threw themselves into the moat, and entered the ravelin by the breach the mine had created. By a stroke of good luck, the engineer Renegat has saved in the city by informing the Governor of all their preparations. To this end Kimpler had placed two mines

[16]George Kimpler

under the same location where the Turks had lodged themselves. These mines were detonated, and many Turks were killed. The survivors did not lose heart but could not hold the ravelin and fell back to the counterscarp, where they defended themselves for a long time. They also remained masters of a communication gate to the ditch. It was necessary for Baron Walter to launch a sortie at the head of some companies of the Württemberg Regiment. It was so sharp and so true that the Turks were surprised in their disorder before they had time to reorganize. They were dislodged and lost 1,500 men. An incident occurred that merits recounting. A Janissary, who was among the first to attack, but was one of the last to retire found himself in the middle of a troop of Germans who wanted to take him prisoner. He refused to surrender and defended himself with desperation. He sabered the first two men that approached him. He wounded several others before he succumbed to a thousand wounds and left the world with an illustrious example of courage worthy of admiration. The Turks were no sooner chased out than the garrison repaired the breaches with new works. And I must not omit to say here that I observed this throughout the siege. The garrison showed itself very prompt in making repairs and entrenchments such that if the Turks took an inch of ground, they could not take a second because after taking the first they always found himself facing new fortifications to attack.

After the assault of the 8th, the Turks took no rest and gave the garrison none either. Four days later, at 2:00 a.m., they came out of their lines and attacked with impetuosity all the locations that they could approach in order to diminish our forces. However, their principal effort was against the point of the ravelin between the Castle Gate and the Lyon Bastion. The furies of hell would not have been worse than what faced Vienna. Thus, everyone fought, everyone distinguished themselves, and no one did anything until it was necessary afterward. It was a very critical day for Vienna. We saw women and children, after having taken refreshments to the combatants, mix with them and having nothing more to do, threw stones at the Turks. Those who threw explosive devices caused great carnage. The grenadiers did even more. The principal officers encouraged their men to fight on, leading their soldiers into the fray where they opened the way with their swords. However, nothing compared to the great Starhemberg. He spared himself so little that he had to perish a thousand times, if Heaven had not wished to preserve Vienna; and if he had been less exposed Vienna surely would have been lost. For, notwithstanding this incredible resistance, the Turks entered by the sap into the moat, and of 2,000 Turks stationed there, only five or six escaped. The battle ended at 5:00 p.m., having lasted without respite for nearly 15 hours and being fought with unusual ardor and constancy. The Turks finally settled on the counterscarp and made themselves masters of a bastion.

The engineer Kimpler, who had already died from a musket shot to the head, rendered after his death, one further service to his homeland, which tore the glory of this day from the Turks' hands. A mine was detonated that he had prepared under the bastion that the Turks had captured. There were easily 2,000 Turks buried under its ruins. Its effect was so great that the others were chased from their posts by the Starhemberg and Mansfeld Regiments, who had already done a thousand wonderful actions during the battle of that day. They launched a sortie which assured the garrison of victory.

The success of this extraordinary counterattack was most glorious and useful for Vienna. Nine or ten thousand Turks remained on the battlefield and the garrison's losses were much lower. But though numerically our losses were low, we had to regret the loss of Count Leslie, Baron Gottlinsky, and the proud Kimpler. The Count von Souches was mortally wounded, and Baron Walter and Count von Starhemberg were also wounded. These great men were all the defenders of the fortress, and there is not one of them, to whom we do not owe a separate relation of the exploits that he had made during the siege. The death of the illustrious Kimpler was worthy of the genuine regrets that this great city showed him, and the praise which posterity will consecrate to his memory will be less than the important services he had given and which he was prepared to render to his country. It was left to Count von Starhemberg to reassure the spirits of the city as nothing had caused so much fright as his being wounded, about which a thousand different rumors spread, so he traveled on horseback through the principal streets, striving to show a joyous and contented face. If he had only this wound, there would have been no reason to be sad. It was only an arrow that touched his face but fell on his shoulder almost without a blow. It is not yet time to touch the reasons that worried him, the fear of dealing with the attacks of the Turks, which they launched one after the other.

On the ramparts the victorious Governor of Vienna heard brass bands of the instruments of war playing as much to revive the garrison as to discourage the Turks. If they passed it in a gloomy silence, as if to give a public avowal of their defeat and the sadness they felt in it, the next day at daybreak they did not fail to return in the attack, sword in hand seeking to erase the shame

of the previous day by at least regaining the posts they had lost. In fact, they lodged themselves first at the foot of the breach of the ravelin, by which they had launched the last assault. They attacked with great fury, and even drove the defenders out; but it was not for long. As soon as the Turks ceased to pursue them, they rallied, returned again, and returned to the same place, whence they had just been repulsed.

Ottoman Spahis (Austrian National Library)

By opening the earth for their trenches, for their mines, and for their other works, they took care to push the excavated earth before them, and at length they formed mountains that turned the counterscarp on the side of their attack. This work was extremely damaging to the garrison. The Turks began to cut these mountains of earth and easily dug a pass by which they descended four times before they could be completely chased out. It was necessary to make wells to the foundations at the point of the ravelin and around the bastions with respect to the main attack. Other works were added to these. These prevented the Turks from advancing, but they always remained in their posts, lodged on the edge of the counterscarp. During the night of 14 August, the Turks descended into the moat before the Lebbel Bastion and dug an entrenchment where neither the cannon nor the garrison's musketry could strike them, because of the depth of the moat and the height of the mountains of excavated earth. By this means they advanced forward, such that the entrenchments that the Imperials made, could not put them in sufficient security. To remedy this by the most efficient means, the Governor had cannon aimed at these new mountains and the next day had them attacked with sword in hand. After an hour of combat, the Turks were forced to retire. The victorious garrison also found itself forced to do the same because they had not brought along sufficient pioneers to destroy these works. That evening, with more people, they ruined more and the following night, under the cover of a successful sortie, they completely ruined them with fire which was fanned by a violent wind, consuming the gabions and galleries of the Turks.

The Grand Vizier then ordered that all attacks on the side of the ravelin stop and he had several mines detonated. The first was fired on the 17th under the ravelin between the Chateau and the Lyon Bastions. It had little effect, because the shells fell behind it and damaged little. Another made a breach in almost the same location and by the breach opened a path to the enemy, who threw forward about 1,000 elite troops, supported by many more. Continuous fire was executed against them with cannon and musketry, which killed more than 300 and obliged them to abandon the breach. They then established a lodgment at the foot of the ravelin. The next day, the 19th, the Turks advanced from the foot of the ravelin towards the demi-lune between the Scottish Gate and the Court Gate and they attacked with such vigor that they were already in possession when the garrison detonated a mine under the demi-lune. Over 600 men were buried and put the remainder in such confusion that they fled when attacked by sword and pike from the position and those they had gained the other day. However, the Grand Vizier, who commanded this attack in person, sent forward a force of 8,000 Janissaries when the initial assault force began to recoil. These new troops, which were fresh, obliged the Imperials to make extraordinary efforts. All the positions were covered with the horrible vestiges of the Turkish fury and our resistance – mounds of bodies and rivers of blood. I will pass over several incidents, which would have place in a more extended relation, than can be done in this letter. The bounds of this letter must not be so narrow, that it cannot contain one admirable accident, which happened to a Janissary, among a thousand others, whose luck spared him from the effects of a mine. This Turk had his just stepped on a stone, going up to the demi-lune, when the fire, violently coming out of the earth, threw him and the stone behind our ramparts into a quagmire, where he found himself without any other evil, then to be scorched.

Whilst the Ottoman army was drawing its way to a general assault, of which it made a great noise, and which was to contain, as it was said, with 50,000 combatants, on the 22 August. Finding themselves in a better position, the Turks had again redoubled the terrible thunder of all their heavy batteries almost without pause from the 13th. For his part Count von Starhemberg prepared himself with all possible care to withstand their assault with honor. He had already given orders for an entrenchment and a ditch had been made in the middle of a ravelin, where the combat had so often been fought. At the Lebbel and Court Bastions, double entrenchments had been made. Behind these two bastions an entrenchment had been constructed to serve as a defense, if the Turks should take possession of it. In addition, he was working on other things, but it was not the Turk against whom this vigilant governor had the most precautions to take; it was the very people, for whose salvation he gave himself so much trouble.

The inhabitants of Vienna were being ground down by the length of the siege and to take up the matter a little farther, they had been assailed for some time at the location, which they feared as the only one capable of causing them to lose. By this I mean by sickness, and by the wound of their governor. His dysentery had lasted nearly 15 days, and whatever he did to hide this from the rest of the world, his face soon gave him away. When the poor people, who had no hope but, in his conservation, perceived a fatal pallor on so dear a face, their consternation was the same, as if they had seen the Grand Vizier come in an assault, iron in hand, and master of their destinies. When the blood drained from his face it rendered this pallor even more redoubtable (as the people never contemplate to examine whether an evil is light or not), you would say that everything universally had been hurt by death's last blow. It is quite true that when Count von Starhemberg was cured of both evils, there was no one who seemed to return with him to his former state. The spirits were allowed to think that the fortress was not impregnable, since the Governor was not immune to the accidents or infirmities of human nature. The continuous vigils, for more than a month, which faced the frequent alarms, and the perils they had experienced were wearing on the bourgeois. The number of their dead, which grew daily, and among which everyone wept for someone, whom nurturing, or friendship made him dear. Dysentery, which began to carry off 50 to 60 men per day, and among them many officers and important individuals. In addition, the bad state of the cannon, of which a great number had been destroyed by the enemy or had burst after being fired too often as well as the long delay of the anticipated relief took its toll. Finally, the terrible threats of an irritated Turkish general, the preparations for a general assault, and the approach of the decisive moment of their destruction; all these things presented themselves at once, and finding courage, which had already been emasculated, put them into a very weakened situation.

However, they continued to endure. They had an abundance of bread, wine, and other food, which were sold at a reasonable price. A pound of meat cost up to 14 sols. They had not lost any of the fortification's works. Only a few houses and a bit of the Imperial palace had been damaged by the Turkish cannon and bombs. All the breaches had been repaired and the Governor, who everyone thought invincible, was well. But some cowardly traitors, who had the ability to pass over to the Turks during the confusion of the attacks, seduced by vain hopes, acted to sell out the city. They insinuated themselves secretly among the population. They amplified the reasons for fear. They exaggerated the kindness with which the Turks treated those who submitted to their empire and their cruelty towards those who held out to the last extremity. They gained so many men that finally, this evil became contagious and extremely dangerous. The time for a prompt and effective remedy was needed.

Only the wise and valiant Count von Starhemberg could deal with this, and he did it with boldness and success. During the morning of 18 August, profiting from a pause in the siege given him by the enemy, he imprisoned two burghers, who were universally judged to be the most seditious. He ordered everyone to assemble in the Neumarkt and, with a face full of pride, he seemed to be in a state of anger, which rendered him infinitely redoubtable, and he spoke in the tone of a man who feels himself to be the master of those to whom he speaks. He made this speech, which I have too well retained, not to insert here:

"Gentlemen, I have known with an extreme sadness for a long time that some miserable mutineers, perverted enemies of the homeland, wish to drag with them into the last misfortune those who have preserved by their valor that has been so far preserved. Nevertheless, I hide my feelings. But they continue and they are listened to. They talk of surrender. Why gentlemen? Do not your vows, your oaths, your past actions make you ashamed, that you dare not admit them? The state of the fortress frightens you; can you not defend yourselves? The anticipation of new enemy forces makes you despair, so you hasten to prevent it [by surrender?], and to evade it? We threw back the last efforts of 200,000 barbarians for a whole month. We have nothing left to chase away, but some nasty remnants, which disappear every day. We have kept our ground, without losing an inch. All our fortifications are complete where, if there is one or two works damaged, the repairs we have made to them make them stronger than those which have not been touched. More than 120,000 arms are coming and applaud us for our glorious resistance and will help us finish it with an even more glorious victory. And we talk about surrendering? Why? Our numbers are diminished. Is that of our enemy augmenting itself? If some brave men among us have died, they ask that you support their honor and that you avenge

their deaths. And having not the patience to preserve two or three days, which they have assured you by their blood, would you wish to negate the beauty of their death, and lose the fruit of your vigils by an eternal reproach? But you are not good enough; no doubt the enemy does it better, and you are reduced to something more horrible than eating the carrion of the horses, as they do? Think well, how infamous it would be to you one day, if it were said that Turks have suffered so much as to feed on the food of dogs and crows, yet they take your life, and to extinguish the name of Jesus Christ. And that you Christians, in order to preserve each other, did not wish to deprive yourself of the delicate pieces. For gentlemen, what do you miss? Dysentery lights up in the city. Well, I advise you to throw yourself into the hands of the infidels, who do not have sufficient captives, to bury those who die by the thousands every day of the same evil in their camp. At last your work has lasted too long. In fact, they would last less if the Vizier was the master of your lives. Gentlemen, you know the Turks. We have killed more than 50,000 of their soldiers. We will leave them only our corpses."

Afterwards extended this thought; then he explained the manner in which the auxiliary troops took to raise the siege, and he thus concluded:

"Finally, gentlemen, we have done well enough to desire to crown our glory by holding on for a few more days. We have mistreated our enemy too much and can hope of nothing from his clemency. Those who are armed for our succor, it is too near, not to wait for it. We must conquer; it depends only on you. If you do not want to be victorious, you have only to die. But God willing, in Vienna one will die only at the breach, or on gallows. For whosoever speaks more of surrender, be he burgomaster, or simple artisan, he will die, but of the kind of death, of which you will now see paid, by these two infamous villains."

At that time, he commanded to bring forward two of the prisoners and they were hung. The execution was done in the sight of everyone and it fortified the impressions of the preceding harangue. The motivation was to do well or to die trying.

That same evening, while the application of the assault provided cover, he sent Prince Charles an officer of the Heusler Regiment dressed as a Turk, and the next day he sent another, disguised as well, to the Emperor, to warn both of them, that in the present state of affairs, it was time that relief came. Then, after a close inspection of all the fortifications, he had mattresses and ox-hides hung on the towers of the bastions and walls, where it was likely that the most violent effort might be directed. He also ordered a large quantity of iron gratings, to be thrown in the manner of a harrow, into places where there would be a breach. He forgot nothing that might raise the spirit of the garrison and whip them into such a state as to beat back a general assault by the Turks.

In the meantime, news was received in Vienna, by means of which one passed from the remnant of terror (for it had not yet ceased) not only to hope, but also to a certain confidence. On the one hand it was learned that Count Castelli, Governor of Neustadt, had defeated a Turkish raiding party, and freed many Christians from captivity; that Colonel Heusler had discovered another that had gone near Turnerfeld seeking grape leaves for forage in the camp, had defeated them, and captured 400 horses and 100 camels. General Dünewald[17] had beaten 4,000 of the malcontents who ravaged Moravia, and killed some 2,000 along with their commander, Colonel Ersedy. The garrison of Raab and that of Comorre had cut off a convoy of 4,000 wagons and had pillaged much of it.

To these successes was added that the Duke of Lorraine's army had been so enlarged by the arrival of part of the troops from the circles, and when no more were coming it could have forced the Turkish lines, if the council of the Emperor had not judged it was more expedient to await the junction of all the armies, in order to obtain a more complete victory; that this junction was to be made at Krembs, or besides the other provisions and war supplies, there was flour for more than 100,000 men for about six weeks. His Imperial Majesty appeared from Passau on the 25th of the current month to go there on the 27th with the Princes of Waldeck and Baden; that the Electors of Bavaria and Saxony; and all the princes in Germany, who had already arrived

[17]Johann Heinrich von Dünewald (1617 – 1693)

there, or were on the road for that purpose; that the Polish army
had marched on the 9th by three different routes. Finally, the King
of Poland, with Prince Alexander, his eldest son, had left Cracow
on the 3rd and when all his troops were united, they would form
a body of more than 26,000 fresh fighters.

We also knew that the decision had been made to relieve
the city by the Vienna Woods or by a boat bridge which would
cut the Danube at The Tabor between the city and the woods;
or by Pressburg, or by Markfeld between Pressburg and Vienna.
The relief would be attempted on the 30th; and to facilitate everything the Count de Leslie, General of Artillery, held himself vis-
à-vis the Vienna Bridge where he maintained communications
between the two banks of the Danube; General Dunewald fortified with troops from Vienna was to carry the Vienna Woods and
level paths there; and the Prince of Lorraine was camped on the
Mark River where the reinforcements anticipated by the Grand
Vizier were to pass with the objective of stopping them.

This news, some of which had already been mentioned,
without considering them in their proper sequence, being now
all collected in the minds and received in a different manner,
produced the effect expected of it. The arrival of Count Albert
Capara at His Imperial Majesty, who was yet to come, was only a
little relief. It was said with much emphasis that, while the Turks
had been in the habit of fearing nothing, they had closed up very
tightly and now that they seemed to show signs that that their
pride had been greatly belittled.

Neither prisoners, spies, nor our own eyes could show us
the true state in the Turkish camp. Combat, sickness, and deser-
tion had taken more than 50,000 from their numbers. A Janissary
assured us that in the single assault of 12 August the Turks had
lost 11,000 dead, including the Pashas of Mesopotamia and Al-
bania; that there was an extreme lack of food; that the best use of
horses was for food; and that the rumor was rife that if the convoy expected from Buda did not arrive soon that famine alone
would raise the siege. Dysentery was ravaging their ranks. The
stench of the dead and the sick had obliged the generals to move
their army to new quarters, so far from the others, that they appeared to be separate camps, but one could easily force the one
before it could be supported by the closest.

The Grand Vizier was enraged by the failure of his attacks and suffering with the anticipation of the coming Christian army to relieve the city. Nonetheless he did not lose heart and resolved to risk everything, be it to anticipate this relief force to strike the last blow, which he had attempted so many times earlier. To this end he ordered Count Thököly and Count Budiany to come with their troops to reinforce his camp. He had also written the Pasha of Buda to send him, for the same purpose, all the soldiers he could, but he had not sent any. In addition, a letter from the Sultan arrived, in which, according to the common rumor, he found a precise order to launch the final assault and then, if it failed, to raise the siege. To complete his misfortunes, he found himself embarrassed by the lack of Janissaries, the best and greater part of which were dead from battle or sickness. What remained was not enough for his purposes. Irritated, but not beaten down by these last new difficulties, he took the step of having his Spahis dismount and used them to fulfill the duties of the Janissaries. In order not to let us pass without incident, which usually accompanies the changes, or perhaps, in order to surprise us at the time we did not expect it, he commanded a frightful assault a day sooner than the rumor had suggested. This assault was launched 21 August.

We spent the night of 20/21 August listening to the continual thunder of the Turkish cannon. A few hours before daylight, the sound of various military musical instruments and the cries of thousands of Turkish warriors reached our ears. In effect, in a few moments the new infantry, or dismounted cavalry, came at us, who, to save themselves in their demotion, because of the superiority they claimed to have over the Janissaries, they demanded to lead the attack. They claimed that if they had marched there in the past, it would not have been necessary to attack again. After the Spahis came those of the Janissaries who could fight, desiring to dispute at least their bravery with those to whom they had been compelled to give way. Then came a few battalions of the troops subordinated to the Porte, between which one was composed of recently arrived, malcontented Hungarians. All determined to prove by the effusion of their blood to their new master, that they were worthy to serve him. It was in this order that these troops marched, sword in hand, over the counterscarp, then the ditch on to the point of the ravelin. They then divided into three parts, some moving against the Lebell Bastion, others against the Court Bastion, and others against the neighboring demi-lune.

In all these locations, where it was thought that the Turks would attack, Starhemberg had assigned capable men who were resolved to well-receive them. In addition, all things necessary for the defense in such situations had been moved to those points. Everyone animated their companions, and everyone was animated by the view of the enthusiasm that was on everyone's face.

At last, in the manner that had been prepared by both sides, to assail and to repulse. It is doubtless that the Turks had been awaiting this day, the one that would render them masters of Vienna; and that those of Vienna regarded this as the day that would deliver them from such a long and redoubtable a siege. Neither of them obtained their wished-for end, because they did all that was necessary to obtain it. Their fine actions were an obstacle to them. The garrison repulsed with too much bravery to be forced, and the besiegers supported themselves with too much courage to be defeated.

When the Turks were within range, the musketry of the fortress saluted them, and the grenadiers threw fire to illuminate them. But nothing was capable of stopping them. Then came the sword fight. That lasted for some time after which the Spahis did not hold as firm as they had promised. Schaffemberg and Württemberg proved that the Imperials could fight better than the Janissaries had believed. The Janissaries, instead of losing heart at the retreat of their companions, seemed to have recovered it as soon as they understood it. It was necessary sooner or later that they suffer the same fate as the Spahis. Their post was the most dangerous for the city and because of this Count von Starhemberg almost always fell on them, but did the means remain to him to resist them? The other troops engaged in a long, bloody action, gaining the upper hand. Meanwhile, the Hungarians came within two fingers of taking the city.

Since a traitor publicly declares himself a traitor, be it to gain universal approval at the time when he does not repent, or be it to compel the consciousness to remain silent, by obstinately contradicting it by his conduct; or by a type of despair, which, when made always precipitates him from one misfortune into another greater yet, it is certain that there is no parallel fury to his own, especially if he may exercise it against persons offended by his treachery. This reason was bound to await the rebellious Hungarians; but they had another perhaps more powerful one. This was jealousy, which has always been between them and the people of Austria, and which has increased much since the interest of religion has been mixed with it. Agitated by two furies, they executed blindly what these furies inspired. They did not stop at anything. They always went on. They pierced everything. They established a lodgment on the demi-lune. They executed great carnage there, and we saw them almost on the point of snatching from fortune in spite of herself, an avowal for the blackest of all their crimes.

What on another occasion would have been a tragedy for the city was, on this occasion, a source of its good luck. The meanest of our troops opposed to those of the enemy, which fought the most furiously, was better than what the best could have done. Do you believe it? Our militia, the burghers had the honors on this memorable day. They were possessed, like the discontented Hungarians, with two terrible emotions: jealousy and one that I do not know what to call. This monster was composed of hatred, indignation, and rage which reinforced their extreme violence against the traitors who had betrayed them. Fury opposed fury, exploding passions in the hearts of the most cowardly and produced the greatest military virtues.

It was above all on the demi-lune that the Hungarians' and the Austrians' rage was the greatest. Swords clashed for hours without breaking ranks. Then, forgetting all discipline and obeying no law but their rage the two enemies mixed together. They moved from sword blows to grabbing collars and dragging each other about. Some were noted rolling together down the demi-lune then climbing up to repeat it shortly later. And it appears, in the way they went, that it would have been necessary to wait to see who would have remained the last on the battlefield, to recognize the victorious party. But at the first moment of the response of the other attacks, the arrival of the Governor caused the staggering victory to turn to his side: his courage aided the new troops that he brought, to stop the Hungarians; his authority then induced the Viennese to rally, and his conduct completed everything. He joined the restored militia with the rest of the people he had with him and even though the Hungarians, also supported by a few new battalions, returned at the charge, they were compelled to retire and not return.

I do not know how to describe this day. It was a general mode of assault to take all action together. In considering its parts, which had some separation, there were six different assaults, or rather it was only a continuous assault, to which they returned six times. But whatever the name one may give it, all that I have to say to you is that it would have been a very pleasant sight to see an infinity of other peculiarities, which I have omitted, if one had been able to be a spectator, as tranquil and indifferent as a reader, who has in his hands the account of some battle. There were few of the enemy in a condition to fight, who found no occasion to distinguish themselves. At the same time and by the same place, they were repelled, and came back to the attack, that is to say, that while some folded under, the others, fresh, succeeded them. When they were broken, others supported them. Works were lost and regained. Among these many retreats and attacks were seen the various corps of an army, sometimes separated, sometimes mixed together. Often the confusion was so great, especially when the Hungarians were fighting, that the enemy was indistinguishable from friends. When fighting the Turks, it was possible to make this distinction, as there was more distinction between the clothes of the Christians and those of the Muslims.

The Grand Vizier commanded his people in person; he sometimes led the first ranks. Then he awaited them at their retreat to make them return from whence they came. If they were either too weary or too hasty, he was careful to furnish them in time with fresh reinforcements; he encouraged them with praise and reproaches, by threats and promises; and in violent agitations, where he sometimes allowed himself to be carried away, he gave a more shameful death to many who fled from the enemy, in order to avoid an honorable one.

The great and indefatigable von Starhemberg did still better than the general of the Ottoman army, because he executed first all that he commanded, and that whatever he commanded, he commanded almost nothing by his actions. Why cannot I give myself a little leeway here? What prodigies of valor, and what admirable effects of his example would you not see? But I must confine myself to the brevity I promised you.

This celebrated action lasted until nightfall. The true number of dead cannot be known. Some claim the Turks took 24,000 prisoners, but others put the number at half that. The besieged would have been in the habit of shedding many tears for such a number and consideration of their loss, if the joy of having escaped from a peril so pressing, even at such a price occupied their minds.

From that point on the Turks engaged us every day and fought only with their swords. They descended into the moat twice, the first vis-à-vis the Lyon Bastion and the second near the Castle Bastion. Our continuous fire prevented them from gaining any ground and the reinforcements sent to us, at the moment they pressed us, forced them to withdraw. Thus, we profited from all our advantages to burn the works that they had constructed in order to fortify their posts and advance them.

A battle between Austrian Hapsburgs and Ottomans (Wikipedia)

At the same time as they attacked us with swords, they particularly battered our walls with cannon. On the 21st, 22nd, and 23rd, the thunder of the cannon was incredible. They also pushed forward their mining effort and detonated some of them under the ravelin and the counterscarp of the palisade. They presented themselves at those breaches with the same impetuosity as usual. They were driven back with the sword and held at bay until the breach was repaired.

The reasons which made them redouble their efforts, served us also as motives for redoubling our own. They were afraid that they would soon be on the arms of the Christian army, and they wanted to take the fortress before it arrived. We hoped it would arrive on the first day, and we wished to risk everything, but while the people and the garrison relied on this hope, the Governor became concerned.

His miner heard the Turkish miners working under the Castle Bastion and it was not doubted that they had not passed the moat. He tried in vain to locate the Turkish mine, but he could not. On the other hand, he saw that the Turks had made an entrenchment that strong enough to put a post in security. The Turks abandoned this mine and turned to another. Hence our miner rightly concluded that someone in the city had contact with them and had warned them of everything. Sooner or later this intelligence might push him to some dangerous extremity. He had devoted all his attention to searching for the authors, but without discovering anything. Thirdly, though the garrison was master of the palisade and the ravelin, with the exception of the point where the Turks were lodged, the palisade had been destroyed by a mine, and the other posts had been heavily damaged by the mine or by cannon fire, so that if the evil arose, the garrison would have lacked the people, either to work on repairs or to repulse the assaults. Dysentery and the daily fighting reduced the garrison's numbers every hour. Fourth: The Turks pressed the garrison more keenly, sparing nothing and hazarding all. It would take only the slightest failure in an attack, and all would be lost. Finally, the auxiliary troops had often deceived the garrison by their delays; Having no certain news, how could it be assured that no further delay would occur?

All these reasons brought von Starhemberg to send, an officer on the 27th, to the Prince of Lorraine with a letter in which he explained his situation, adding that he could not long wait for relief. Two days later he sent a similar dispatch to the Emperor. At almost the same time he acted to reduce concerns.

The Vizier of Buda, according to the order mentioned earlier that he had received from the Grand Vizier, had sent him 10,000 Turks, under the leadership of the Pashas of Javarin and Agria. They were joined on their march by 3,000 Tartars, who had the son of the Great Khan at their head. After they crossed the Danube at Gran, they encountered Count Thököly with the Hungarians. Together they formed a corps of 15,000 to 16,000 men. This force crossed the Mark River in good order and without obstacle, then advanced to Pressburg, a league from Vienna. Prince Charles of Lorraine (who had left the Mark River after having rested there a few days waiting for the Turks, as I had mentioned earlier) was then on the road from Closter-Neuburg moving to the general rendezvous of the Christian army. As soon as he was advised of the movement of these enemy troops, he resolved to fight then and sent three Polish regiments of Chevalier Lubomiski and two regiments of German cavalry to observe them. The Poles executed more than their commission. They attacked the Turks as soon as they saw them. They also paid dearly for their disobedience. They were received with vigor and broken almost at the same time. They rallied, however, several times, and tied up the combat for a long time. But in the end, as the battle went badly for them, they were obliged to retire to the main body of the Imperial army, which the Prince of Lorraine had put into battle formation. The Turks pursued them there and in the force of their impetuosity, they pierced the first and second lines, which were the vanguard, and where the squadrons of cuirassiers were all put in disorder. At the third line, which was the beginning of the battle corps, the dragoons took the lead and gave the others time to recognize themselves. After this, the battle changed its face.

Fortune passed on the side of the Christians, and the Turks went over to the defensive. They were charged on all sides with the artillery, musket fire, and with the sword. They did defend themselves, the two pashas especially, who, on this occasion, wished to efface by some singular feat the shame of the defeat at Pressburg, which, it was said, resulted from their bad conduct; these two pashas, moved among their soldiers and captains, such that if they had been imitated, or obeyed, this second rout would not have been so complete. But the Tartars soon fled towards Markfeldt. The Turks also fled, part moving towards Vienna and part towards the Mark River. There was only Count Tekely, who retreated in good order before the Poles. The Imperial army was master of the battlefield and split up to pursue the fugitives. On one side, as far as the Vienne Bridge, they hotly pursued those who were withdrawing from it. On the other side, they pressed the Turks so closely much towards the Mark River where more than 300 were drowned. The rest fell into the hands of the peasants, who made a great butchery of them. Prince Charles, who had paid admirably with his person during the battle, set about pursuing Thököly, but the night and the weariness of the horses kept him from doing anything.

This victory could not have been more glorious or more important for the Empire. The defeated had been destined to reinforce the Grand Vizier and to prevent the junction of the Germans with the Poles. They had defeated the best Turkish cavalry, with more than 500 to 600 excellent horses, richly equipped falling into the hands of the Christians along with 22 flags, six kettle drums, 200 prisoners, and about 3,000 dead Turks on the battlefield. Some wished to include among the dead the Pasha of Waradin and Agria. Others say that the son of the Great Khan had drowned. What is certain is that three Christian generals were wounded and the number of wounded greatly surpassed the dead. However, this did not cost the Christians much. Among the wounded were the Marquis de Doria and a colonel, but there were few dead.

As soon as Count von Starhemberg received this news, he had it published throughout the city. To it he added that after his victory he heard that the Prince of Lorraine had gone to encamp at Closter-Neuburg to wait for the King of Poland. King had left his wife, the Queen of Poland, on the 22nd at Tarnouitz and that he would join at the Imperial army on the 27th accompanied by fresh troops consisting of an illustrious nobility accustomed to defeating the Turks. He also said that the Emperor would be leaving Linz on the 25th for Krembs, where Cardinal Bonuisi, in the capacity of nuncio and papal legate, would bless the flags of the army and distribute sums that His Holiness had provided for the war. He also said that Count Serau, with his corps and a body of Croats, had defeated the rebellious Hungarians, under the leadership of Count Budiany, that had moved into Styria and that the Croats had then moved into Lower Hungary to ravage, in their turns, the hereditary lands of Count Budiany.

Although all this news raised the hopes of a certain and prompt delivery of Vienna, they brought no joy to the Governor as great as a small incident. The various spies that he had put in search of the individual who had given the Turks the information relating to the state of the fortress, were caught in the early morning during a fight when he attempted to return from the camp. In a matter as important and as delicate as that, this presumption was sufficient to question him under torture. In the midst of this torment he confessed that he was an Italian, the son of a distiller who had long been a regular in Vienna; that he had gone five or six times to the enemy, but that he had not involved himself with any other intrigue than to inform the Turks of the state and strength of the city. His confession was followed by the execution he deserved. He was hanged from the wall on the side of the Ottoman camp, so that the Turks might learn on seeing him that it was difficult to surprise the vigilance of a governor such as ours. A few days later, a new subject arose that restored him to his first sense of tranquility. The diligence of his miner in digging under the Castle Bastion was so pressing, that he met the mine which was so frightening. It was the finest work that could be done in this matter. Had this mine exploded it would have resulted in the fall of Vienna and the Turks were ready to exploit this. Our good fortune saved us this time. And, by a situation entirely opposed to its intent, it proved of great advantage to us. In anticipation of the success of the mine, the Turks had also half-filled the bastion's moat with fascines. It was necessary for us to take away this remnant of an advantage. Fortune seconded our efforts, and we ended the month of August with a feu de joie that ignited and burned up all these fascines.

The beginning of September brought us to the last point where fears and hopes were equally well founded and made us feel the most violent attacks of these two troublesome and turbulent passions. The Ottoman army pressed us with extreme pressure, with mines, cannon, and continual attacks. The main battery was against the gate and the Scottish Bastion. Mines were exploded under the Lyon Bastion and the Castle Bastion. Assaults took the end the moat and the ravelin which was between these two works. On the 7th, the Turks thought they could push their lodgments further. A mine exploded under the Lyon Bastion. It was as effective as they wished. They presented themselves at the breach, saber in hand, launching an assault with all the fury and relentlessness that human force is capable of. The indefatigable Starhemberg, by his singular art of inspiring with his ardor all who approached him, inspired women and children as well as soldiers and captains. Extreme danger threatened our lives.

For the Turk was well before the fortress and only our swords could dispute their entry. The ravelin in which he had been lodged, and the two neighboring strongholds, were all destroyed by mines and the trenches, and resembled nothing but piles of accumulated ruins, and freshly turned earth. Besides, the bastions were so narrow within, that as it was difficult to get back to them for want of earth, we looked upon them as abandoned. If there had been only that, we could have continued to fight. But of all that is necessary for the defense of a besieged city, we lacked everything, food and ammunition, artillery, and soldiers. Food was becoming scarce and the meat (which the Germans could not do without like the French cannot do without wine) was available only at an excessive price. We had only very little powder and almost no lead. Forty cannons had been dismounted. The siege had resulted in the death of 15,000 soldiers of the garrison and 10,000 to 12,000 of its inhabitants. The rest were wounded or sick (because dysentery was increasing) or entirely exhausted. Our combatants were reduced to a number incapable of resisting the new attacks. People most inappropriate for war were filling the gaps in the ranks of the defenders. Finally, Vienna was at a point where it could not stand without the hope of relief and the exhaustion of the Turks.

Relief was certain, but it was slow. The King of Poland was, on 27 August, at Wolfersdorf, a few leagues from here beyond the Danube. From there, by the return of Count Carassa, who had been sent to him at Tarnowitz from where he wrote to the Emperor that he would come after he had made his testament, because he was resolved to spare neither his blood or live for the salvation of the Empire. On the 31st, he received Prince Charles of Lorraine and the Prince of Waldeck, who he had come to see. On 1 September, he paid them a visit at Sterdorf, a league from Tuln. On the 3rd, after Prince Herman of Baden, President of the Imperial Council of War, had come to him on the part of His Imperial Majesty (who, in order to avoid the embarrassment of civilities had broken his plan to join the army) he held a council of war with all the generals and princes of Germany (who had come from everywhere to the rendezvous to share the honor of such a glorious occasion and under the command of a prince of such an extraordinary reputation). It was decided that His Polish Majesty would command the right wing; that the Prince of Lorraine with the Duke of Saxony would command the battle corps, and that the Elector of Bavaria would command the left wing with the Prince of Waldeck. All the troops would cross the Danube on the 6th and Vienna would be relieved on the 10th. It was decided that they would approach Vienna through the Vienna Woods. To this end boat bridges were constructed at Krebs, Tuln, and Sterdorf. They were wide enough to permit the passage of four horses abreast or eight infantrymen abreast. Soon afterwards a detachment of the army moved to reconnoiter the Vienna Woods where the Turks had entrenched themselves with some artillery to amuse the Christians. They were chased out.

The Grand Vizier was as well informed as we were and could not be further embarrassed. Count Thököly, the Prince Abasi of Transylvania, the Hospodars of Moldavia and Wallachia did not appear, and the rumor spread that the last three did not know the part they were to play. The Janissaries, who counted among their rights, that they could not be obliged to serve before a fortress for only forty days, that they had already spent more in the siege of Vienna, and being extraordinarily repelled by having been so ill-treated, mutinied and would not continue fighting. In addition, the camp was in a pitiable condition, not sufficiently entrenched against a numerous army which came to attack it, it was divided into sections that were too far apart from each other to be defended and reduced to a small number of already exhausted fighters.

It is true that the general of the Turks acted here as a great captain, who, by an art most useful in human affairs, instead of letting himself be abased by the disgrace of fortune, knows how to profit from it, or at least to remedy it. He again summoned the four princes whom I have just named, ordering them to come to his army under penalty of death. With a little skill he appeased the Janissaries. Prisoners told us that he had negotiated an agreement with them, that they should serve four days longer, one in consideration of the Sultan, the other in his name, the third in the name of their aga, and the latter for money; Assuring themselves, as was true, that before they had come to this end their boredom would have passed away, and that the attitude of the mutineers would be changed. Then he assembled and brought out his troops. He made the lines of circumvallation work to defend his works against the Christian army. He entrenched himself strongly on all sides of his camp. In order to prevent an entrance, he again placed artillery in the avenues with which he had beaten our walls, and, in order not to be surprised in the retreat which he foresaw as inevitable, he sent his heavy artillery and most embarrassing baggage to Hungary.

The Turks arrayed themselves to us in battle order at once, at an enemy camp in very bad order, but still pursuing its efforts toward the besieged city which was reduced to the last extreme, trying to hold on for another two or three days. There was a powerful fresh army which was coming to its assistance, but which might perhaps be too late. By a thousand different imaginations like so many phantoms, half beautiful and half frightful, the latter pushing on one side, those repulsed by another pitilessly breaking hearts and weary only of sad relics of their cruel combat and extraordinary confusion. Never in the most violent of winds had the sea beheld in its foaming waves so much fury, that the spirits felt themselves carried away at one and the same time by impetuous and opposing agitations, by fear, the confidence of hope, and despair.

But because, in this ebb and flow, which confounds agreeable passions with the disagreeable, they are not only more acutely felt by the common people but are poisoned by their bitterness what is deceived in others. The greater part of the Viennese, who had fallen prey to and were entirely abandoned to the rigors of fear and despair, were not touched either by the confidence they had in the relief force or the hope that it would come early. These concerns alone could increase their unbearable anxiety. It was an image very foreign to consider and too difficult to represent in this afflicted city. Vienna saw the uncertain fate of her last destinies fall before her, so to speak, and that as soon as this fatal extremity arrived, everyone who followed her blindly took a different impression, particular inclinations occurred in each one, and words became the mirrors exposing the most chaste feelings without any personal thought that one might have another prudence to guard. From time to time it happened that there were as many concerns and opinions as people; it was a confused tumult, where one could see absolutely nothing.

The Governor forgot nothing to sustain the steadfastness of the poor inhabitants or to procure them a prompt delivery. He frequently sent dispatches to the Emperor and Prince Charles. He fired rockets and set signal fires on the St. Stephan Tower, signals that had been agreed would be made when he could no longer hold out.

In the meantime, a detachment of cuirassiers or dragoons and infantry descended on boats to one of the islands in the Danube within view of Vienna. They chased out the Turks and signaled Vienna. Though the siege had provided me many examples of happiness among the people whose emotions were in constant flux, I had never thought to see, as on this occasion, such a rapid movement from one emotion to another. Those who at the first thought themselves entirely lost now thought only of engaging the Turks in favor of this detachment. The arrival of an envoy from the Emperor brought more joy as he reported that the Prince of Baden had assured His Imperial Majesty that everything was ready for the relief of the city; that the first corps was in route via Maurbach and Maur, the battle corps was moving on Volkersdorf, and the rearguard on the side of Closter-Neuburg and Nusdorf.

The certain assurance that help was at hand did not fail to be disturbed by several alarms. Those of the Turkish cannon that remained continued to fire. They were relentless in pressing their work, in continuing their attacks, advancing their posts, and gaining ground. While these efforts were resisted, the idle people went to the highest part of the city to see if the Christian army was coming, and because there were continual movements of troops in the fields, sometimes they cried out that it was the relief force and sometimes it was new enemies that were arriving. On the 10th without being seen the number of the Turks had grown. The Grand Vizier ordered Prince Abassy and the two Hospodars (who obeyed his last order) to stand between Gran and Vienna in order to protect his retreat, had brought forward the pasha who had previously held this post with 12,000 soldiers and having grown his army with this corps, and several others whom he had also called, he was in a position to be able to continue the siege and to repel the Christian army.

There was another change of scene. The day of the antic-ipated relief had passed, the city believed that it was no longer able to continue, and there was nothing to hope for from the Turk, who had been driven to extremity. Only despair seemed to possess our hearts, but this did not last.

The battle of the standard (Jozef Brandt, 1905)

On the 11th, a certain signal was received from the Vienna Woods. During the morning of the 12th the Ottoman army, after having left the lines that protected it and allowed them to push the siege, came into sight. I will leave it to your imagination the eagerness of the inhabitants in contemplating a spectacle already so agreeable, as uncertain as it was, if the denouement would be happy. They thought of nothing but watching the pending show. The Governor warned everyone: "That the salvation of the city did not depend only on those who had come to relieve it, but that, while they were conquering on one side, in order not to lose the fruit of their victory, it was necessary that they should take action against those who remained in the camp."

In fact, by the order of their general, he made the batteries continue firing. They exploded a mine, to prepare for an assault, and they already started moving when, without waiting for them, the Viennese struck them in their posts with a sortie, to received them firmly at the breach. The Turks fought, as if they were fighting to the death, and the besieged fought like those who, in a shipwreck having long fought with the waves, found themselves with only a short swim to get into port. The attack was so hot and so tumultuous that almost no one in the battle took notice of what was happening in the camp itself until one heard a thousand and one voices shouting together from the ramparts, that the succor was there, and that the Turks were defeated.

I must now take up the matter a little farther. But because in the heat of victory where one still stands, one cannot really know the truth of all the particularities, each one telling them in his own fashion. I will avail myself of the resolution which I have made of writing nothing but what is certain, in order to acquit myself of the engagement in which I have begun to be as short as possible.

On 11 September, Colonel Heusler had opened the passage in the Vienna Woods and had established a position on the Kalemberg. On the 12th, the Imperial army marched out under cover of this post before sunrise, advancing very slowly towards the city because it lacked its artillery, which was two hours away. A detachment of Turkish infantry supported by a large force of cavalry came forward with horrible cries and fell on the troops of the Prince of Lorraine. This valiant general received them with all firmness possible, pushed them back in their turn, and obliged them to retire on the battalions that had not yet fought. Those battalions helped the Turks rally and return at the charge. They engaged the Bavarians and Saxons, commanded by their electors. The advantage would have been long disputed except for the arrival of the Prince of Waldeck, who came with the troops of the Franconian Circle. The Turkish cavalry fled, leaving their infantry to the merciless considerations of the Christians.

The Grand Vizier arranged his other troops in battle formation on the Vienna Mountain. He stopped the fugitives from the first battle and rallied them only to have them defeated a second time. The Germans, seconded by the Poles fell on them suddenly from various directions and pushed their point with such vigor that even though the Turks defended themselves, rallied, and did everything that one can expect of soldiers on the point of being defeated, they were, nonetheless, defeated and fled towards their camp.

The Imperials did not pursue them as much to avoid disorder as out of fear of mines ready to be exploded in the avenues of the Turkish lines. However, after the grenadiers had scouted the enemy and the pioneers opened pathways, the Grana Regiment, the Baden Regiment, and one of dragoons, following the Prince of Lorraine, who with sword in hand marked their path, pierced the first ranks, cutting through the first ranks, passing through the tents, and fell on the Turks that were engaged by the sortie by the Viennese. At the same time, the King of Poland with his troops, who were almost all armored and armed with lances passed through the quarter of the Grand Vizier and cut through everything as far as those who were facing the walls of Vienna. There they encountered 700 or 800 Janissaries, who ceased fighting the garrison and turned to face the Poles, who tore them to pieces. This last action put an end to the siege of Vienna.

Stanislaw Potocki (Wikipedia)

At this point the whole of the Ottoman army had fled, the cavalry being first, which had not fared well. The infantry, who had suffered the greatest slaughter, for a long time, thereafter, was mounted on wagons, which the Grand Vizier had previously allocated for that purpose. They were already out of the line, such that those who worked at the mines did not know what was happening over their heads and had not yet emerged from below ground. They were massacred, and their deaths increased the number killed on this day to some 8,000 men. We bought the battle cheaply - Duke Maximilian von Croy and Count von Transmandorf were mortally wounded along with few others of consideration. The Poles suffered almost as few as us. The most illustrious of their dead is a relative of the King from the House of Potocki.[18]

After this fortunate outcome, our governor went to His Polish Majesty and the other generals giving respects on one side and appreciation on the other, and praise for all for this difficult undertaking which were difficult to hear among the cries of joy from the city and the songs of victory from the army.

These things were, however, soon interrupted by the order from the chiefs. As the Turks had not retired in such great disorder that they could not return to their camp at night, and could surprise the Christians, the generals of the army commanded the soldiers to remain in their own quarters as in the presence of the enemy, and forbade, under pain of death, looting neither the tents nor the dead. The Governor of Vienna also ordered the garrison and inhabitants of the city to be in the same position as if there were to be an assault on the morrow.

Early the next morning, 13 September, the King of Poland, accompanied by Prince Alexander, his son, some senators, and other lords from his kingdom entered Vienna among the acclamations of all the people, who in the transport of their infinite joy praised his glorious name to Heaven. He went directly to the Augustins where they solemnly sang the *Te Deum* before Our Lady of Lorette. Upon leaving he was splendidly treated, along with the Dukes of Bavaria and Saxony by Count von Starhemberg and upon rising from the table he placed himself at the head of his troops and the light German cavalry, to begin the pursuit

[18]Stanisław Potocki (1659-1683)

of the Turks. He caught up with and engaged part of their rear-guard, taking from it some artillery, some horses, and baggage, which included much silver.

That same day the Imperials pillaged the Turkish camp taking an infinite booty, wagons loaded with food and baggage, horses, camels, oxen, cattle, tents, money, 100 large and small cannons, and everything that the Turks took with them when they went to war, plus what they had amassed in their pillaging. The King of Poland took the tent of the Grand Vizier and his equipment. He found immense riches there, among other things, his fine golden weapons adorned with diamonds, a beautiful battle horse, and the most superb harnesses one could imagine. He already had the Turkish Great Standard, which he presented to the Pope. The sick who had remained in the camp, numbering 700 to 800, were burned to death in their quarters as a reprisal for the act of the Grand Vizier in killing the Christian prisoners who could not follow him quickly enough in his retreat.

Prince Alexander Sobieski

Before the end of the day Count von Starhemberg went to Closter-Neuburg where the Emperor had gone before the battle. His Majesty greeted him as would be expected after what he had done for the Empire. After words of praise, he presented him with a considerable sum of money, 10,000 florins, promoted him to the rank of maréchal de camp[19], promised him the necklace of the Golden Fleece, and several other things.

Before he left the city, he issued orders to prepare it for the Emperor's entrance. Work was done through the night to achieve this. The next day, 14 September, was consecrated in the

---

[19]Translator: Maréchal de camp may or may not have been the actual title, as this is a French rank and the equivalent of a brigadier general.

church dedicated to the memory of the triumphant entrance into Jerusalem by the Emperor Heraclius, after having conquered an infidel prince, who was the curse of the Christians of his time. We were spectators of the magnificent victory of His Imperial Majesty over the most formidable enemies the Church had ever had.

He descended along the Danube and when his boat was observed it was saluted by a discharge of all the cannon and the musketry of the city. When he wished to land, there was a second salvo like the first, and the Dukes of Bavaria and Saxony with their guards in their livery, several of the principal officers of the army, the Magistrate of the city, and the people of Vienna were there to greet him. The burghers under arms formed a double row from the bridge to St. Stephan's Church and the garrison was on the bastions or ramparts as they had been during the siege.

Though the honors were for the Emperor, but one could also say that this triumph was for Count von Starhemberg. When they saw this incomparable man by His Imperial Majesty's side, he was greeted as one of the heroes of antiquity who had descended from Heaven. Almost all the looks and applause were for him. He was called the "Liberator of Vienna, "The Savior of the Homeland," the "Conqueror of the Ottomans" and a thousand other honorable names that expressed the high esteem and marvelous appreciation that everyone had for the valor and extraordinary wisdom he had shown in pulling the Viennese from a peril where without him they would have invariably lost their lives and liberty. This ceremony occurred in the Cathedral where a *Te Deum* was sung to the sound of a third discharge of cannon and musketry, the ringing of all the clocks of the city, and with the greatest solemnity as had been seen in Germany for many years. From the church the Emperor went to the Archducal Palace (the Imperial palace having been made uninhabitable by the siege). After dining he gave a public audience in which he promised immunities to the Viennese and considerable presents to the garrison.

The next day, on 15 September, he visited the army posted two hours from the city. He passed first to the Bavarians where the Elector of Bavaria received him with his sword in hand, which had been a gift from His Imperial Majesty some time before, and they gave mutual greetings.

    After reviewing the German troops, the Emperor approached those of the King of Poland. The King advanced on his horse and, both being mounted, they embraced each other in a most fraternal manner, spoke for a quarter of an hour, and then separated. The King of Poland placed himself at the head of his army and His Imperial Majesty, accompanied by the most illustrious Polish lords, passed through the Polish ranks.

    After the first reflection which the inhabitants of Vienna had been able to make on what appeared before their eyes around their walls, there flowed torrents of tears. Indeed, they wept for some dear person lost and for the ruin of their country-houses, the ravage of their lands, and the desolation of their property. When they had no part in all that they saw, it was still a theater too frightful of all the horrible disasters of fortune, not to show their distress by tears. More than two or three leagues around all was desecrated, destroyed, burned, and covered by a vast and frightful road of human corpses exposed as stinking carrion.

Sobieski at Vienna (Juliusz Kossack, 1882)

    This is the subject of universal joy in all Christianity. However, more than 100 leagues of country were ruined, more than 500 villages or towns were burnt, 400,000 to 500,000 men died or were made captives; 60,000 to 80,000 Turks were dead, 20,000 to

25,000 Christians are also dead, all Germany has been exhausted, and extraordinary festivals were held everywhere. And it is true, however, that for a century there has been no reason to do so. There is vanity, even in the most solid foundation of human rejoicing.

After such a long letter, I should have made a hundred apologies to you, which would bother you even more. To avoid it I reduce them to two. The first one is about what I did not tell you about me. I did not think I should. It would make me very happy to communicate to my good friends, but we must reserve this pleasure at our first meeting, it will be more agreeable. You know the engagements where I am, and the employment that I have here. That's enough for this time. In the second place, though I am not capable of great perfection in the art of writing well, you will have to take up many more things which I might have avoided if I have not been so rushed. What do you want? I ventured to write to you poorly, to write you quickly, believing that novelty was preferable to politeness. I hope also that your curiosity will win the forgiveness of my faults with your delicacy.

From Vienna, 25 September 1683.

Jan Sobieski meeting the Emperor on the field at Vienna (Jan Grottger)

Personas and Groups

Prince Michael Apasi of Transylvania (1632-1690) was elected with the support of the Ottomans by the nobles of Transylvania in 1661, in opposition to the Habsburg-backed ruler John Kemény. He opposed the Holy Roman Emperor Leopold I, supporting the Ottomans and Hungarian rebels until the Ottoman defeat at the Battle of Vienna on 12 September 1683. Eventuall, Michael opened talks with Leopold and concluded a treaty with the Austrians on 27 September 1687 to confirm his authority in Transylvania.

Prince Herman of Baden-Baden (1628-1691) was a general and diplomat in the imperial service. At different times he was Field Marshal, president of the Hofkriegsrat, and the representative of the Emperor in the Perpetual Diet of Regensburg. After 1679, Hermann again acted as the Emperor's envoy to various courts. In 1682, he succeeded Montecuccoli as president of the Hofkriegsrat. In 1683, he travelled to Hungary, to prepare for the Great Turkish War when he was appointed field. When the Turkish army approached Vienna, Hermann requested permission to stay in the city, but was only granted one day to clean up affairs. During that day, he managed to help make some preparations for the defense of the city. On 3 September 1683, he represented the Emperor in a meeting of the great council of war, with King John III Sobieski of Poland and other allies. At this point Charles V of Lorraine took command of the imperial troops. During the Battle of Vienna, he was positioned on Mount Kahlenberg, close to the King of Poland. Although he was initially intended as a reserve, he stormed down the hill and attacked to Turkish troops at his front. He captured many trophies, which he later bequeathed to his nephew Louis William (nicknamed Türkenlouis).

Stefan Báthory (1533-1586) The son of Stephen VIII Báthory and a member of the ruling Hungarian Báthory family. Báthory was a ruler of Transylvania in the 1570s, and in 1576 Báthory became the third elected king of Poland by marrying Anna Jagiellonia He worked closely with chancellor Jan Zamoyski who had married his niece. He was forced to spend the first years fighting off rivals to the throne including Maximilian II, Holy Roman Emperor, and squashing rebellions. He is considered one of the most successful kings in Polish history, particularly in the realm of military history. His signal achievement was his victorious campaign in Livonia against Russia in 1582, which he repulsed a Russian invasion and secured a highly favorable treaty of peace (the Peace of Jam Zapolski).

Marcin Broniowski (early 16th C – 1593) a courtier in the court of King Zygmunt August who belonged to the Catholic camp and signed a protest against the Warsaw confederation (first European Act granting religious freedom to all – 1573). During the court of King Stefan Bátory he was the court secretary. He was a Polish envoy to the Perekop Khan, Mahmed Giray in 1578 and negotiated a peace agreement between them. The next year he was sent back to the Tatars. In 1580 he returned and spent the following years in the royal court. After the death of Stefan Batory, returned to demand repayment for expenses from the legation to the Tartars. During the electoral parliament he was a supporter of a Piast candidate but agreed to Sigismund. Prince of Conti, Louis Armand de Bourbon (1661-1685) served with distinction in Flanders in 1683, and, against the wish of the King, went to Hungary, where he helped the Imperialists defeat the Turks at Gran. He died at the Palace of Fontainebleau from smallpox, which he contracted from his wife.

Charles of Lorraine (1643-1690) spent his military career in the service of the Habsburg Monarchy; he played an important role in the 1683-1696 Turkish War that reasserted Habsburg power in South-East Europe and ended his life as an Imperial Field Marshall. Although the Treaty of Nijmegen confirmed his title as Duke of Lorraine France retained the territory and in 1681, they also annexed the Alsatian capital of Strasbourg. He was appointed Commander of the Imperial army during the Great Turkish War in 1683. He was outnumbered by the Ottomans were also supported by anti-Habsburg Hungarians known as

Kurucs, as well as non-Catholic minorities who opposed Leopold's anti-Protestant policies. Charles positioned his men outside Vienna, shielding them from the plague epidemic then prevailing in the city and killed many of the Ottomans besieging it. He focused his forces on raiding the Ottoman camps and protecting resupply convoys to the city, the Pope gathered support for the Habsburgs. This was eventually known as the Holy League. Led by John III Sobieski, in combination with Charles's troops they defeated Ottomans at the Battle of Vienna on 12 September 1683. In the next few years, the Habsburg army under Charles recaptured large parts of Hungary; the most significant victories being the Siege of Buda in 1686 and the Second Battle of Mohács in 1687. He returned to command Imperial forces in the Rhineland, where he died in 1690.

Baron Hannibal von Degenfeld (1648-1691) was the youngest son of the well-known general Christoph Martin von Degenfeld. He became a soldier like his father and his brothers and first saw action under the Elector Johann Georg III of Saxony. From 1674 to 1677 he was colonel and commander of a foot regiment. Von Degenfeld left the Electoral Saxon army and entered the service of the Elector of Bavaria, who appointed him Field Marshal Lieutenant and President of the Hofkriegsrats in 1682. The following year, he commanded the 12,000 auxiliary troops against the Ottomans, distinguishing himself in the relief of Vienna. At the end of the campaign he took service in the Republic of Venice against the Ottomans in the Peloponnese.

Count Paul Esterhazy (1635-1713) was the first Prince Esterházy of Galántha from 1687 to 1713, Palatine of the Kingdom of Hungary from 1681 to 1713, and an Imperial Field Marshal. He participated in various battles against the Ottoman Turks during the Fourth Austro-Turkish War (1663–1664) and the Great Turkish War (1662–1669).

The House of Giray a dynasty that reigned in the Khanate of Crimea from its formation in 1427 until its downfall in 1783. The dynasty also supplied several khans of Kazan and Astrakhan between 1521 and 1550. Before reaching the age of majority, young

Girays were brought up in one of the Circassian tribes, where they were instructed in the arts of war. The Giray khans were elected by other Crimean Tatar dynasts, called myrzas (mırzalar). They also elected an heir apparent, called the qalgha sultan (qalğa sultan).

Jagiellonians were a royal dynasty, founded by Jogaila (the Grand Duke of Lithuania, who in 1386 was baptized as Władysław, married Queen regnant (also styled "King") Jadwiga of Poland, and was crowned King of Poland as Władysław II Jagiełło. The dynasty reigned in several Central European countries between the 14th and 16th centuries. Members of the dynasty were Kings of Poland (1386–1572), Grand Dukes of Lithuania (1377–1392 and 1440–1572), Kings of Hungary (1440–1444 and 1490–1526), and Kings of Bohemia (1471–1526). The personal union between the Kingdom of Poland and the Grand Duchy of Lithuania (converted in 1569 with the Treaty of Lublin into the Polish–Lithuanian Commonwealth) is the reason for the name "Poland–Lithuania". After the death of the last male of the line Sigismund II (Sigismund Augustus) his sister Anne Jagiellonia was elected ruler and married Stefan Báthory. Following his death, she advocated the election of Sigismund III, son of her sister even though she could have ruled outright.

Janissaries were elite infantry units that formed the Ottoman Sultan's household troops, bodyguards and the first modern standing army in Europe. The corps was established during the reign of Murad I (1362–89) from impressed young Christian boys who were converted to Islam. They were famed for for strict discipline and order. Unlike typical slaves, they were paid regular salaries. Forbidden to marry or engage in trade, their complete loyalty to the Sultan was expected. By the seventeenth century, due to a dramatic increase in the size of the Ottoman standing army, the corps' initially strict recruitment policy was relaxed which eroded their military élan. The corps was abolished by Sultan Mahmud II in 1826.

Emperor Leopold (1640-1705) was Holy Roman Emperor, King of Hungary, Croatia, and Bohemia. Following the death of his elder brother Ferdinand IV he was elected Holy Roman Emperor in 1658, and ruling until his death in 1705. Leopold's reign is known for conflicts with the Ottoman Empire in the east and rivalry with Louis XIV, a contemporary and first cousin, in the west. Under the Treaty of Karlowitz, Leopold recovered almost all of the Kingdom of Hungary, which had fallen under Turkish power in the years after the 1526 Battle of Mohács. Leopold fought three wars against France: the Franco-Dutch War, the Nine Years' War, and the War of the Spanish Succession.

Louis XIV of France (1638-1715) was a monarch of the House of Bourbon who reigned as King of France from 1643 until his death in 1715. Louis XIV's France was a leader in the growing centralization of power. An adherent of the concept of the divine right of kings, which advocates the divine origin of monarchical rule, Louis continued his predecessors' work of creating a centralized state governed from the capital. He sought to eliminate the remnants of feudalism persisting in parts of France and, by compelling many members of the nobility to inhabit his lavish Palace of Versailles, succeeded in pacifying the aristocracy, many members of which had participated in the Fronde rebellion during Louis' minority.

Hieronim Augustyn Lubomirski (1648-1706) was a Polish noble, politician and famed military commander. He was a Prince of the Holy Roman Empire. Son of Grand Marshal and Hetman Jerzy Sebastian Lubomirski he was first Great Chorąży of the Crown in 1676, Court Marshal of the Crown in 1683, Grand Podskarbi of the Crown in 1692, voivode of Kraków Voivodeship, Field Crown Hetman, castellan of Kraków and Great Crown Hetman in 1702. Under the command of Jan Sobieski, he fought against Tatars and Turks and participated in the expedition and siege of Chocim in 1673. He refused to join the "Lubomirski Rebellion" of his father in 1665-1666. As Marshal he led the ordinary Sejm on January 10 - May 21, 1681. He took part in the Vienna expedition in 1683 and the following campaigns in Hungary. In the Royal election of 1697, he backed up the candidature of Prince Conti for the Polish throne. He supported the Warsaw Confederation in 1704 against August II and the proclamation of interregnum, in the hope that he would gain the Polish crown, with the help of Sweden. He went into retirement from political activity, after the election of Stanisław Leszczyński.

Archduke Maximillian of Bavaria (1662-1726) became elector in 1679. By 1683 he had embarked on a military career, fighting in the defense of Vienna against the attempt of the Ottoman Empire to extend their possessions further into Europe. He returned to court for long enough to marry Maria Antonia, daughter of Leopold I, Holy Roman Emperor in 1685. In 1688, he led the capture of Belgrade from the Turks, with the full support of Serbian insurgents under the command of Jovan Monasterlija.

Leopold Philip Fürst Montecuccoli (1663 – 1698) was an Austrian Field Marshal and son of the famous Imperial Field Marshal Raimondo. After his father died in 1680, he took over command as Colonel of his Cuirassier-Regiment and became later Field Marshal-Lieutenant. He also became captain of the Imperial Trabanten-Leibgarde, Geheimrat and Knight in the Order of the Golden Fleece

Riamondo Montecuccoli (1609-1680) was an Italian-born professional soldier who served the Habsburg Monarchy. He was also a Prince of the Holy Roman Empire and Duke of Melfi, in the Kingdom of Naples. Montecuccoli was considered as the only commander to be the equal of the French general Turenne, (1611–1675), and like him, was closely associated with the post-1648 development of linear infantry tactics

Kara Mustapha Pasha (1634-1683) He served as a commander of troops in a war against Poland, negotiating a settlement with Jan Sobieski in 1676 that added the province of Podolia to the empire. The victory enabled the Ottomans to transform the Cossack regions of the southern Ukraine into a protectorate. When his brother-in-law Köprülü Fazıl Ahmed Pasha died that same year, Mustafa succeeded him as grand vizier. Kara Mustafa led several successful campaigns into Ukraine, attempting to shore up the position of the Ottoman vassal Cossack state of Right-Bank Ukraine. He established Ottoman garrisons in many of Ukraine's cities, and conquered the traditional Cossack capital of Chyhy-ryn. In 1683, he launched a campaign northward into Austria in a last effort to expand the Ottoman Empire after more than 150 years of war. By mid-July, his 100,000-man army had besieged Vienna (guarded by 10,000 Habsburg soldiers), following in the footsteps of Suleiman the Magnificent in 1529. By September, he had taken a portion of the walls and appeared to be on his way to victory. But on 12 September 1683, a Polish army under King Jan Sobieski took advantage of dissent within the Ottoman military command and poor disposition of his troops, winning the Battle of Vienna with a devastating flank attack led by Sobieski's Polish Winged Hussars. The Ottomans retreated into Hungary, much of which was subsequently conquered by the Habsburgs and their Holy League allies. The defeat cost Mustafa his position, and ul-timately, his life by strangulation with a silk cord.

Hermann Otto II of Limburg Stirum (1646-1704) In 1678 he was named commandant of an imperial regiment. After his nomina-tion as General-Major in 1684 he distinguished himself several times in the wars against the Ottomans and becoming a Field Marshal in 1696. in 1701 he fought in the War of the Spanish Succession in the service of the Holy Roman Emperor Leopold I against France and Bavaria. In 1703, he lost the Battle of Höch-städt against the French-Bavarian forces under General Villars. In 1704, he led the second assault on enemy positions in the Battle of Schellenberg and was mortally wounded. He died a few days later.

Feliks Kazimierz Potocki (1630-1702) He was the son of Hetman and magnate Stanisław "Rewera" Potocki and brother of Hetman Andrzej Potocki. He married the daughter of Hetman and Mar-shal of the Crown Prince Jerzy Sebastian Lubomirski in 1661. He was Podstoli of the Crown from 1663, voivode of Sieradz in 1669, Voivode of Kiev in 1682, Voivode of Kraków in 1683, Field Crown Hetman in 1692, castellan of Kraków and Great Crown Hetman in 1702. He fought in wars against Cossacks, Sweden, Transylvania and Muscovy from 1655 to 1664. As the Marshal of the Election Sejm on 2 May – 19 June 1669 in Warsaw, he contributed to the election of Michał Korybut Wiśniowiecki as King of Poland. He became famous in the Chocim expedition in 1673. He signed the sejm's election document of Jan Sobieski as King of Poland and participated in the Vienna expedition in 1683 during Great Turkish War. He fought against Tatars and Turks in many battles. In 1698 the Polish army under his command, completely smashed the Tatar expedition to Poland in the battle of Podhajce.

Stanisław Potocki (1659 –1683), was the starosta of Halicz and Kołomyja, rotmistrz and pułkownik of cavalry. Son of Hetman Andrzej Potocki and brother of Hetman Józef Potocki.

Sigismund Augustus (Sigismund II) (1520-1572) Sigismund was the only legitimate son of Sigismund the Old. In 1529 he was crowned King while his father was still alive. He reigned was one of relative peace and stability; considered as the apex of the Polish Golden Age. In 1569 he oversaw the signing of the Union of Lublin between Poland and the Grand Duchy of Lithuania, which formed the Polish-Lithuanian Commonwealth and introduced an elective monarchy. Sigismund Augustus was last male member of the Jagiellon. Following the death of his sister Anna in 1596 the Jagiellonian Dynasty came to an end.

Sigismund III (1566-1632) King of Poland and Grand Duke of Lithuania, monarch of the united Polish–Lithuanian Commonwealth from 1587 to 1632, and King of Sweden (where he is known simply as Sigismund) from 1592 until he was deposed in 1599. He was the son of King John III of Sweden and his first wife, Catherine Jagiellonia of Poland. Elected to the throne of the Polish–Lithuanian Commonwealth, Sigismund sought to create a personal union between the Commonwealth and Sweden (Polish–Swedish union) and succeeded for a time in 1592. After he had been deposed in 1599 from the Swedish throne by his uncle, Charles IX of Sweden, and a meeting of the Swedish Riksdag, he spent much of the rest of his life attempting to reclaim it. Sigismund took advantage of a period of civil unrest in Muscovy (known as the Time of Troubles) and invaded Russia, holding Moscow for two years (1610–12) and Smolensk thereafter. In 1617 the Polish–Swedish conflict, which had been interrupted by an armistice in 1611, broke out again. While Sigismund's army was also fighting Ottoman forces in Moldavia (1617–21), King Gustavus II Adolphus of Sweden (Charles IX's son) invaded Sigismund's lands, capturing Riga (1621) and seizing almost all of Polish Livonia. Sigismund concluded a truce with Sweden in 1629 and never regained the Swedish crown. While initially supported by Jan Zamoyski, Sigismund's focus in the Swedish crown and creating a hereditary monarchy alienated the minister.

Sipahi/Spahi were two types of Ottoman cavalry corps, including the fief-holding provincial timarli sipahi, which constituted most of the army, and the regular kapikulu sipahi, palace troops. Other types of cavalry which were not regarded sipahi were the irregular Akinci ("raiders"). The sipahi formed their own distinctive social classes, and were notably in rivalry with the Janissaries, the elite corps of the Sultan.

Alexander Sobieski (1677-1714) was a Polish prince, nobleman, diplomat, writer, scholar and the son of John III Sobieski, King of Poland. He accompanied his father to Vienna Campaign and several other military campaigns. He was a candidate for election to the Polish throne in 1697, following his father's death, but was unsuccessful. In 1702, he declined Charles XII of Sweden's offer to set him up as a rival king to Augustus II of Poland. He died in Rome in 1714 after becoming a Capuchin friar.

Jan Sobieski (1629-1696) was one of the most successful and powerful military leaders of Poland against a myriad of enemies. Sobieski's reign was marked by a period of stabilization, after the turmoil of the Deluge and the Khmelnitsky Uprising. He fought in many campaigns against the Cossacks and the Ottomans. He rose through the ranks to Grand Hetman of the Crown in 1667 and won a great victory over the Ottoman's at Khotyn in 1673 which propelled him to the kingship. His victory at Vienna and subsequent one's against the Turks led to an infusion of booty into the Commonwealth that initiated a period of eastern fashion. After his victories over them, the Ottomans called him the "Lion of Lechistan"; and the Pope hailed him as the savior of Christendom

Ernst Rüdiger Graf von Starhemberg (1638-1701) was military governor of Vienna from 1680, the city's defender during the Battle of Vienna in 1683, Imperial general during the Great Turkish War, and President of the Hofkriegsrat. In 1683 he was military commander of the city of Vienna, with fewer than 20,000 men to oppose about 120,000 besieging Ottomans. On 12 September, 80,000 Polish, Venetian, Bavarian, and Saxon troops finally attacked the Turks and were able to defeat them in the Battle on the Kahlenberg. Starhemberg was promoted to the rank of a field marshal and minister of state by the Emperor, recognizing his action in saving the capital. Starhemberg was severely wounded in 1686 during the ensuing campaign at the Siege of Buda; by a shot in his left hand. In 1691 he was made President of the Hofkriegsrat and was responsible for the organization of the Habsburg army.

Imre Thököly (1657-1705) was prince of Upper Hungary from 1682 to 1685, and prince of Transylvania in 1690. His father, Count István Thököly, held large land grants in Royal Hungary. His mother was related to three princes of Transylvania and when he was a child when he inherited his mother's estates in Transylvania proper and the domains of his uncle, Count Francis Rhédey, Prince of Transylvania. István Thököly was involved in the leading aristocrats' conspiracy against the Habsburg monarch, Leopold I, and died fighting against the royal troops in late 1670. Imre fled to the Principality of Transylvania and his estates in Royal Hungary were confiscated. He continued to lead opposition to the Hapsburgs and tried to raise revolt during the Ottoman's invasion.

Wasa was the name royal house founded in 1523 in Sweden, ruling Sweden 1523–1654, the Polish-Lithuanian Commonwealth 1587–1668, and the Tsardom of Russia 1610–1613 (titular until 1634). John III married a Catholic Polish princess, Catherine Jagiellon, leading to the House of Vasa becoming rulers of Poland. Their Catholic son Sigismund III Vasa, then ruler of a short-lived Polish–Swedish union, was usurped in 1599 by John's Protestant brother King Charles IX of Sweden in the War against Sigismund. The dynasty was split into a Protestant Swedish branch and a Catholic Polish one, which contended for crowns in subsequent wars. John II Casimir of Poland abdicated in 1668. With his death, the royal House of Vasa became extinct in 1672.

Winged Hussars - were one of the main types of the cavalry in the Polish-Lithuanian Commonwealth between the 16th and 18th centuries. Modeled on the Hungarian Hussars, the early hussars in Poland were light/medium cavalry of exiled Serbian warriors; by the second half of the 16th century and after Stephen Báthory's reforms, hussars were transformed into a heavily armored shock cavalry. Until the reforms of the 1770s, the husaria banners were considered the elite of the Polish cavalry. In their heyday of the 17th century the Hussars were famous for their huge "wings", a wooden frame carrying eagle, ostrich, swan or goose feathers. In the 16th century, characteristic painted wings or winged claws began to appear on cavalry shields. There are several theories about why they wore the wings but the most plausible seems that they made a loud, clattering noise which made it seem like the cavalry was much larger than in reality and frightened the enemy's horses. Other possibilities included the wings being made to defend the backs of the men against swords and lassos. Winged hussar were the elite cavalry for more than a century and a silhouette of them is worn on some Polish tanks units in World War II and today.

Jan Zamoyski (1542-1605) was a Polish nobleman, magnate, and the founder of the town of Zamość who played a role in every level of Polish governmental and military life in the late 16th and early 17th century. He received various titles including Royal Secretary in 1566, Deputy Kanclerz (Chancellor) of the Crown in 1576, Lord Grand-Chancellor of the Crown in 1578, and Grand Hetman of the Crown in 1581. He was an important advisor to Kings Sigismund II Augustus and Stephen Báthory. He worked on behalf of Anna Jagiellon to support Bathory's successor, Sigismund III Vasa. He orchestrated several successful campaigns including one against the Hapsburgs and the Tartars. He eventually had a falling out with Sigismund over his attempts to create a hereditary monarchy. Zamoyski is recognized as one of the most skilled diplomats, politicians and statesmen of his time, standing as a major figure in the politics of the Polish-Lithuanian Commonwealth throughout his life.

Prince Jerzy Zbaracki (1574-1631) was son of Janusz Zbaracki and older brother was Krzysztof Zbaracki. As part of the court of King Sigismund III Vasa he visited Sweden with him in 1598. Jerzy Zbaraski support the King Sigismund III Vasa during the Zebrzydowski Rebellion of the nobles against his attempts to create monarchical privileges and a hereditary kingship.

Terms & Titles

Agha or Aga - a general officer in the Ottoman Empire.

Bastion - a projecting part of a fortification built at an angle to the line of a wall, so as to allow defensive fire in several directions.

Chancellor - was one of the highest officials in the historic Poland. This office functioned from the early Polish kingdom of the 12th century until the end of the Polish-Lithuanian Commonwealth in 1795. The Chancellors' powers rose together with the increasing importance of written documents. In the 14th century the office of Chancellor of Kraków evolved into the Chancellor of the Crown which eventually became responsible for the foreign policy of the Kingdom and later, the Commonwealth. The Chancellor was also supposed to ensure the legality of monarch's actions, especially whether or not they could be considered illegal in the context of pacta conventa which spelled out the responsibilities of the monarch to the state.

Chiaoux - Envoy of the Ottoman Empire.

Counterscarp - the inner and outer sides of a ditch or moat used in fortifications. Attackers (if they have not bridged the ditch) must descend the counterscarp and ascend the scarp. In permanent fortifications the scarp and counterscarp were often made of stone. In less permanent fortifications, the counterscarp may be lined wooden stakes set at an angle so as to give no cover to the attackers but to make advancing and retreating more difficult. If an attacker succeeds in breaching a wall a coupure (cut) can be dug on the inside of the wall to hinder the forlorn hope, in which case the side of the ditch farthest from the breached wall and closest to the center of the fortification is also called the counterscarp

Curtain Wall – a fortified wall around a defensive work that links towers together.

Hetman - The Polish title Grand Crown Hetman dates from 1505. The title of Hetman was given to the leader of the Polish Army and until 1581 the hetman position existed only during specific campaigns and wars. After that, it became a permanent title. At any given time, the Commonwealth had four hetmans – a Great Hetman and Field (deputy) Hetman for both Poland and Lithuania. From 1585, the title could not be taken away without a proven charge of treachery, thus most hetmans served for life. Hetmans were not paid for their job by the royal treasury. Hetmans were the main commanders of the military forces, second only to the monarch in the army's chain of command. The fact that they could not be removed by the monarch made them very independent, and thus often able to pursue independent policies. This system worked well when a hetman had great ability and the monarch was weak, but sometimes produced disastrous results in the opposite case. The security of the position notably contrasted with that of military leaders in states bordering the commonwealth, where sovereigns could dismiss their army commanders at any time.

Grand Vizier - was the de facto prime minister of the sultan in the Ottoman Empire, with absolute power of law and, in principle, dismissible only by the sultan himself in the classical period, before the Tanzimat reforms, or until the 1908 Revolution

Pasha - was a high ranking official in the Ottoman political and military system, typically granted to governors, generals, dignitaries and others.

Ravelin - is a triangular fortification or detached outwork, located in front of the innerworks of a fortress (the curtain walls and bastions). Originally called a demi-lune, after the lunette, the ravelin is placed outside a castle and opposite a fortification curtain. The outer edges of the ravelin are configured that it divided an assault force, and guns in the ravelin can fire upon the attacking troops as they approach the curtain. It also impedes besiegers from using their artillery to batter a breach in the curtain wall. The side of the ravelin facing the inner fortifications has at best a low wall, if any, so as not to shelter attacking forces if they have overwhelmed it or the defenders have abandoned it. Frequently ravelins have a ramp or stairs on the curtain-wall side to facilitate the movement of troops and artillery onto the ravelin.

Starosta - was a title for the middle nobility, comparable to a baron, as well as an office, corresponding to a district administrator. Until 1795, there were two types of Starosta: Castle-Starost, and Land-Starost; an overseer of crown land tenants or land tenure (see also tenant-in-chief). The first was a representative of the king, chief administrator in the territory or district.

Vizier - is a high-ranking political.

Look for more books from Winged Hussar Publishing, LLC –
E-books, paperbacks and Limited Edition hardcovers. The best
in history, science fiction and fantasy at:
https://www. wingedhussarpublishing.com
or follow us on Facebook at:
Winged Hussar Publishing LLC
Or on twitter at:
WingHusPubLLC
For information and upcoming publications

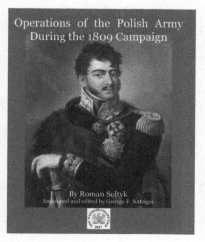

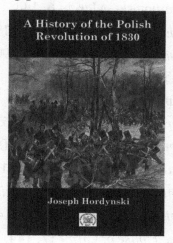

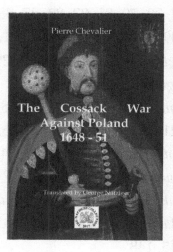

INDEX